GREAT BRITISH CHEESES

SOFT CHEESES
As white rind cheeses ripen, the bacteria in the mold work from the surface of the cheeses inward, causing them to soften from the outside in.

MORNISH ISLE OF MULL

Isle of Mull Cheeses at Sgriob-ruadh Farm Dairy, Tobermory, on the Isle of Mull makes this white mold-ripened cheese, using milk from its own cows. *Penicillium candidum* is added to the milk to create the white bloomy mold coating on the cheese. It is sent out at three weeks, when it is young and firm. As it ripens, the pale yellow paste softens from the outside in. The flavor is mild and creamy.

SIZE	
D. 4½in (11cm) & 8in (20cm)	
H. 1½in (4cm)	
WEIGHT	
1lb 2oz (500g) & 2¼lb (1kg)	
SHAPE Round	
MILK Unpasteurized cow's	
RENNET Vegetarian	
TYPE Modern	

OLD BURFORD SOMERSET

Made by Wootton Organic on its farm and dairy at North Wootton, this mold-ripened cheese uses organic Jersey cow's milk supplied by a neighbor. Traces of the golden rind are visible under the white mold coating, while the paste is a primrose yellow, softening at the edges as the cheese ripens. The flavor, while reflecting the buttery creaminess of the Jersey milk, has a notable salty-sweetness.

SIZE	
D. 4in (10cm)	
H. 1¼in (3cm)	
WEIGHT	
7¾oz (220g)	
SHAPE Round	
MILK Unpasteurized cow's	
RENNET Vegetarian	
TYPE Modern	

PENYSTON GLOUCESTERSHIRE

This organic cheese is made by Daylesford Creamery using unpasteurized organic milk from the estate's herd of Friesians and traditional animal rennet. A mold-ripened cheese, it is rind-washed as it matures, and develops a bloomy white mold coating over an apricot-colored rind. At four weeks, the yellow paste has a chalky texture and a clean, lemony flavor; at six weeks, the texture is voluptuous and the flavor is buttery.

SIZE	
D. 1¼in (3cm)	
H. 4in (10cm)	
WEIGHT	
10½oz (300g)	
SHAPE	Square
MILK	Unpasteurized cow's
RENNET	Traditional animal
TYPE	Modern

PERL WEN DYFED

This organic white mold-ripened cheese is made by Caws Cenarth in Wales. The bloomy white mold rind covers a pale yellow paste, which, as is characteristic of this type of cheese, softens from the outside in. As the cheese ripens, it also develops in flavor. When young, the flavor is very mild and faintly lemony; as it matures, it becomes richer and sweeter with a salty aftertaste.

SIZE	
D. 8in (20cm)	
H. 1¼in (3cm)	
WEIGHT	
4½lb (2kg)	
SHAPE	Round
MILK	Pasteurized organic cow's
RENNET	Vegetarian
TYPE	Modern

PONT GAR WHITE
CARMARTHENSHIRE

This white mold-ripened cheese is made by the Carmarthenshire Cheese Company. The name comes from "Sir Gar," Welsh for Carmarthenshire. It has a thick, even coating of white mold over a smooth, sticky pale yellow paste. As it ripens, the paste softens from the outside. A mild, creamy cheese, it has a faint mushroomy note.

SIZE	
D. 4½in (11cm)	
H. 1½in (4cm)	
WEIGHT	
9oz (250g)	
SHAPE Round	
MILK Pasteurized cow's	
RENNET Vegetarian	
TYPE Modern	

RAGSTONE HEREFORDSHIRE

This soft log-shaped goat cheese is made by Neal's Yard Creamery. When Charlie Westhead started making the cheese, Neal's Yard Creamery was based in Kent, and its name derives from the Ragstone Ridge there. The cheese is molded in pipes, which gives it a characteristic log shape, and has a white bloomy rind and smooth white paste. It has a smooth lactic flavor and is excellent grilled.

SIZE	
H. 2in (5cm)	
L. 6in (15cm)	
WEIGHT	
10½oz (300g)	
SHAPE Log	
MILK Pasteurized cow's	
RENNET Vegetarian	
TYPE Modern	

SHARPHAM DEVON

Made since 1980 by Sharpham Creamery on the Sharpham Estate near Totnes, this is a white mold-ripened cheese using unpasteurized milk from the estate's own Jersey cows. Sharpham is ready to eat at four weeks, by which time it is coated in a bloomy white mold over a smooth yellow paste which is firm when young, softening as it ripens. The flavor is mild and creamy when young, and stronger when ripe.

SIZE	
D. 3¾in (9.5cm) & 7¼in (19cm)	
H. 1½in (4cm) & 1¾in (4.5cm)	
WEIGHT	
9oz–2¼lb (250g–1 kg)	
SHAPE	Square & round
MILK	Unpasteurized cow's
RENNET	Vegetarian
TYPE	Modern

SHEPHERD'S CROOK SOMERSET

As its name suggests, this is a sheep's milk cheese, made by Wootton Organics, North Wootton, using unpasteurized milk from its own flock of sheep. Ready to eat at three to four weeks, this is a mold-ripened cheese with a golden rind blotched with a fine coating of bloomy white mold and a glossy white paste, which softens from the outside in as the cheese ripens. The flavor is clean and fresh.

SIZE	
D. 3½in (9cm)	
H. 2in (5cm)	
WEIGHT	
7¾oz (220g)	
SHAPE	Round
MILK	Pasteurized cow's
RENNET	Vegetarian
TYPE	Modern

SLEIGHTLETT SOMERSET

This small, delicate goat's milk cheese is handmade by Mary Holbrook at Sleight Farm, near Timsbury, Bath. Only a little rennet is used to curdle the milk, so the curd is fragile and requires careful handling. The distinctive black ash coating, sometimes mottled with blue and green molds, covers a brilliant white cheese. The flavor is refreshingly clean and lactic, with a hint of goat; the texture is smooth and velvety.

SIZE	
D. 3in (7.5cm)	
H. 1¼–1½in (3–4cm)	
WEIGHT	
7oz (200g)	
SHAPE Wheel	
MILK Unpasteurized goat's	
RENNET Traditional animal	
TYPE Modern	

ST EADBURGHA WORCESTERSHIRE

A white mold-ripened cheese made by Gorsehill Abbey Farm, this cheese uses milk from the farm's herd. A *Penicillium* mold is sprayed onto the cheeses, which are then matured and eaten at 4–12 weeks, depending on their size. By this stage, the white mold has grown over the apricot-colored rind, while the ivory paste inside is smooth and shiny. Creamy-textured, it softens as it ripens, and has a full, mushroomy flavor.

SIZE	
D. 3½–13¾in (9–35cm)	
H. 1½in (4cm)	
WEIGHT	
6oz–6½lb (175g–3kg)	
SHAPE Round	
MILK Pasteurized cow's	
RENNET Traditional animal	
TYPE Modern	

ST GEORGE EAST SUSSEX

Nut Knowle Farm at Horam makes this white mold-ripened goat cheese using whole milk from its own herd of goats. The bloomy white mold grows over a pale yellow rind, while the paste is pale cream in color. St. George is sold at two weeks, when it is a firm young cheese with only a mild hint of goat. As the cheese ages and ripens, it softens from the outside in and develops in flavor.

SIZE	
D. 4in (10cm)	
H. 1¼in (3cm)	
WEIGHT	
10oz (280g)	
SHAPE Round	
MILK Pasteurized goat's	
RENNET Vegetarian	
TYPE Modern	

ST KEVERNE CORNWALL

Made by the Lambrick family at Toppenrose Dairy, this white mold-ripened cheese uses milk from their Friesian herd. The name is inspired by the nearby village of St. Keverne, visible from the farm. Sold at three to four weeks, the cheese develops a white mold rind over a pale yellow paste, which softens as the cheese ripens. It tastes mild and mellow, with mushroomy overtones.

SIZE	
D. 3¾in (9.5cm)	
H. 1in (2.5cm)	
WEIGHT	
9oz (250g)	
SHAPE Square	
MILK Pasteurized cow's	
RENNET Vegetarian	
TYPE Modern	

ST KILLIAN CO WEXFORD

Carrigbyrne Farmhouse Cheese in Ireland makes this white mold-ripened cheese, named after a Wexford saint, using milk from the farm's own herd of Friesians. *Penicillium candidum* is added to the milk at the start of the cheese-making, and it is sold at 12 days old when it has a bloomy white rind and a pale yellow paste. As the cheese ripens, it softens, developing a melting texture, and it has a milky, mild flavor.

SIZE	
D. 2¾in (7cm) & 4in (10cm)	
H. 1in (2.5cm)	
WEIGHT	
5½oz (150g) & 9oz (250g)	
SHAPE	Round & hexagonal
MILK	Pasteurized cow's
RENNET	Vegetarian
TYPE	Modern

ST TOLA CO CLARE

This soft organic goat cheese is made by Inagh Farmhouse Cheese, Ireland, using unpasteurized milk from the farm's own goats. As it matures, St. Tola develops a distinctively whorled pale gold rind, from the *Geotrichum* mold, over the soft bright white paste. At its best at four weeks, the cheese has a melting texture and a sweet fullness of flavor with a faint, lingering fresh tang of goat.

SIZE	
D. 3in (7.5cm)	
L. 10in (25cm)	
WEIGHT	
2¼lb (1kg)	
SHAPE	Log
MILK	Unpasteurized organic goat's
RENNET	Traditional animal
TYPE	Modern

TOPPENROSE GOLD CORNWALL

Toppenrose Dairy at Trenance makes this little soft cheese using milk from its own herd of Friesian cows. Locally sourced Jersey double cream is added to the milk, resulting in a white mold-ripened cheese with a noticeably golden yellow paste. The cheese is sold at five to six weeks, by which time the smooth paste has softened to a creamy texture, and the cheese has a rich creaminess of flavor.

SIZE	
D. 2½in (6cm)	
H. 2in (5cm)	
WEIGHT	
3½oz (100g)	
SHAPE	Round
MILK	Pasteurized cow's
RENNET	Vegetarian
TYPE	Modern

RENNET

Curdling the milk to separate solid fat and protein from the liquid is an essential part of the cheese-making process. This is most commonly achieved using rennet, a substance containing the enzyme rennin (also known as chymosin). The traditional source of rennet was the lining of the fourth stomach of a calf or other young dairy animal. This lining was salted and dried to preserve its properties, and cut into strips that were added to vats of soured milk to trigger the curdling. Today, animal rennet is available to cheesemakers in liquid or powder form.

Cheesemakers can also use vegetarian alternatives. Plants such as lady's bedstraw (*Galium verum*) or the wild cardoon (*Cynara cardunculus*) have been used in the past to curdle milk, but modern cheesemakers tend to rely on rennet produced from the fungus *Mucor miehei* or the bacterium *Bacillus subtilis*. It is also possible to manufacture chymosin in the laboratory using genetic engineering techniques, creating a substance identical to animal rennet without using calf cells.

TRICKLE SOMERSET

This dainty cheese is one of a range of goat's milk cheeses made by Peter Humphries of White Lake Cheeses at Bagborough Farm, using unpasteurized milk from the farm's herd of Saanen, Toggenberg, British Alpine, and Anglo-Nubian goats. A white mold-ripened cheese, it has an even coating of bloomy white mold over its rind and a smooth white paste. The flavor is mild and sweet with a goaty tang.

SIZE	
D. 2¼in (5.5cm)	
H. ¾in (2cm)	
WEIGHT	
1¾oz (50g)	
SHAPE Round	
MILK Unpasteurized goat's	
RENNET Vegetarian	
TYPE Modern	

TUNWORTH HAMPSHIRE

Similar in style to a French Camembert, Tunworth is a modern cheese handmade on a family farm in Hampshire by Julia Cheyney and Stacey Hedges of Hampshire Cheese, using milk from a local herd of Holstein cattle. The resulting cheese, with its wrinkled white rind, is eaten at between four to six weeks, and has a soft, creamy texture. The flavor is mellow and nutty with mushroomy notes.

SIZE	
D. 4½in (11cm)	
H. 1¼in (3cm)	
WEIGHT	
9oz (250g)	
SHAPE Disc	
MILK Unpasteurized cow's	
RENNET Traditional animal	
TYPE Modern	

TYMSBORO SOMERSET

The natural rind of this goat cheese varies in appearance, coated predominantly with either white mold or green and blue over a fine coating of black ash. It is handmade by Mary Holbrook at Sleight Farm, near Timsbury, Bath, using milk from her own goats. The texture of the paste ranges from creamy soft near the edge to smooth and firm at the center, while the flavor is rich with a subtle tang.

SIZE	
D. 3¼in (8cm) base; 1½in (4cm) top	
H. 3in (7.5cm)	
WEIGHT	
9oz (250g)	
SHAPE	Truncated pyramid
MILK	Unpasteurized goat's
RENNET	Traditional animal
TYPE	Modern

VIPERS GRASS SOMERSET

Strikingly named, this flavored organic cheese is made by Daisy & Co in Somerset. It is a white mold-ripened cheese made from organic Jersey cow's milk, sourced locally. The chopped chives and garlic are added to the milk at the beginning of the cheese-making process. A dainty sprinkling of chives marks the bloomy white mold rind. The pale yellow paste is smooth in texture and has a subtle savory flavor.

SIZE	
D. 4in (10cm)	
H. 1in (2.5cm)	
WEIGHT	
5½oz (150g)	
SHAPE	Round
MILK	Pasteurized organic cow's
RENNET	Vegetarian
TYPE	Modern

WATERLOO BERKSHIRE

Village Maid Cheese makes this at its creamery near Reading using unpasteurized milk from Guernsey cows. The curd is washed, removing some of the acidity, and the molded cheese is brined. Ripened for 4–10 weeks, Waterloo develops a white rind, dusted with mold, and a soft yellow paste. The flavor is mild and creamy when young, and richer and fuller as the cheese ripens and the texture softens.

SIZE	
D. 6½in (16cm)	
H. 1¾in (4.5cm)	
WEIGHT	
1½lb (675g)	
SHAPE Round	
MILK Unpasteurized cow's	
RENNET Vegetarian	
TYPE Modern	

WEALDEN EAST SUSSEX

This small goat cheese is made by Nut Knowle Farm at Horam using pasteurized whole milk from the farm's own flock of British Toggenburg and Saanen goats. When young, the cheese has an ivory-colored rind over a white paste which has a mild, sweet flavor with a goaty tang. As the cheese ages, it darkens in color and takes on a stronger, much more goaty flavor.

SIZE	
D. 2in (5cm)	
H. 2in (5cm)	
WEIGHT	
2¾oz (80g)	
SHAPE Round	
MILK Pasteurized goat's	
RENNET Vegetarian	
TYPE Modern	

WEALDWAY EAST SUSSEX

Nut Knowle Dairy at Nut Knowle Farm, Horam, makes this cheese using whole goat's milk from the farm's own herd of Toggenburg and Saanen goats. The curds are ladled into molds and drained under their own weight. The cheese is a smooth bright white log with a soft but dryish paste with a delicate, slightly goaty flavor. It is also available in flavored versions, coated in herbs or seeds.

SIZE	
D. 2¼in (5.5cm)	
L. 5½in (14cm)	
WEIGHT	
5½oz (150g)	
SHAPE Log	
MILK Pasteurized goat's	
RENNET Vegetarian	
TYPE Modern	

WHITE HEART SOMERSET

This romantic-shaped white mold-ripened soft cheese is made by White Lake Cheeses at Bagborough Farm using milk from its goats. At the start of the cheese-making, the milk is thermized (that is, heated for at least 15 seconds at a temperature between 135°F (57°C) and 154°F (68°C). Ready to eat at three to four weeks, it has a white bloomy covering over a soft, moist white paste and a very fresh delicate flavor.

SIZE	
D. 3¼in (8cm)	
H. 1½in (4cm)	
WEIGHT	
7oz (200g)	
SHAPE Heart	
MILK Thermized goat's	
RENNET Vegetarian	
TYPE Modern	

WHITE LAKE SOMERSET

White Lake Cheeses at Bagborough Farm makes this white mold-ripened cheese using milk from the farm's own herd of Saanen, Toggenburg, British Alpine, and Anglo-Nubian goats. The cheese is matured for between four to six weeks, during which time it develops a fine bloomy white rind over the interior paste, which is smooth and ivory-colored. The flavor is clean with a hint of goat and a long finish.

SIZE	
D. 4in (10cm)	
H. 1in (2.5cm)	
WEIGHT	
7½oz (210g)	
SHAPE	Round
MILK	Thermized goat's
RENNET	Vegetarian
TYPE	Modern

SHEEP'S MILK

Sheep's milk was always the most widely used milk in British cheese-making—it was used, for example, to make Wensleydale (see page 182). As cows, with their high milk yield, became the favored dairy animal, fewer cheeses were made from sheep's milk. Today, however, there has been a revival, with a number of British cheesemakers producing sheep's milk cheese.

Sheep's milk has appreciably more solids in it than either cow's or goat's milk, and is high in fats and protein, allowing for a high yield of cheese from the milk. Sheep's milk is naturally homogenized with the very small-sized fat molecules in the milk remaining evenly mixed throughout, making it easily digestible. Bright white in color, it has a rich, nutty flavor which characterizes many sheep's milk cheeses.

DAIRY SHEEP
Sheep's milk was used in early cheese-making, but sheep were also valued for their meat and wool.

WHITEHAVEN CHESHIRE

Made by the Ravens Oak Dairy at Nantwich, this is a white mold-ripened cheese produced from locally sourced goat's milk. The molded curd is dipped first into brine, to add salt to the cheese, then in a *Penicillium* mold, which creates the dense coating of bloomy white mold over the cheese. The paste inside is white and smooth, firm when young and softening as it ripens, and the cheese has a mildly goaty flavor.

SIZE	
D. 3in (7.5cm)	
H. 1½in (4cm)	
WEIGHT	
5½oz (150g)	
SHAPE	Round
MILK	Pasteurized goat's
RENNET	Vegetarian
TYPE	Modern

WITHYBROOK DEVON

This goat cheese is made for Country Cheeses by Debbie Mumford on the Sharpham Estate. The molded cheese is coated with black ash, a process particularly associated with goat cheeses. Matured for four to six weeks, when ripened, the cheese has a bloomy white mold covering a fine layer of black ash with a gleaming white interior paste. This striking-looking sliced cheese has a dryish texture and a strong goaty tang.

SIZE	
D. 3½in (9cm) base; 2in (5cm) top	
H. 3in (7.5cm)	
WEIGHT	
10½oz (300g)	
SHAPE	Truncated pyramid
MILK	Unpasteurized goat's
RENNET	Vegetarian
TYPE	Modern

SEMI-SOFT CHEESES

With a slightly firmer texture than soft cheese, the semi-soft variety is, to put it bluntly, the smelliest group of cheeses. Washed-rind cheeses are easily identifiable by their powerful odor, sticky orange exteriors, and full-flavored paste. Washed-curd cheeses, with their supple-textured paste, also fall into this group.

ADMIRAL COLLINGWOOD
NORTHUMBERLAND

Named after a Northumbrian naval hero, this washed-rind cheese from Doddington Dairy uses unpasteurized milk from the farm's cows. It is molded and washed in Newcastle Brown Ale as it matures, and it develops an orange rind over a smooth yellow paste. The flavor is full and mellow with a distinctive lingering ale aftertaste.

SIZE	
D. 5½in (14cm) & 7in (18cm)	
H. 1½in (4cm)	
WEIGHT	
2¼lb (1kg) & 4½lb (2kg)	
SHAPE Square	
MILK Unpasteurized cow's	
RENNET Traditional animal	
TYPE Modern	

ADRAHAN CO CORK

Adrahan Farmhouse Cheese in Ireland makes this cheese, using pasteurized milk from the farm's own cows. During cheese-making, the rind is washed with brine. Matured for four to eight weeks, Adrahan develops a sticky, ridged golden-orange rind over a pale yellow paste, dotted with a few holes and a savory aroma. The paste has a creamy, giving texture, and the flavor is mild yet complex.

SIZE	
D. 7½in (19.5cm)	
H. 2in (5cm)	
WEIGHT	
3lb 3oz (1.5kg)	
SHAPE Round	
MILK Pasteurized cow's	
RENNET Vegetarian	
TYPE Modern	

BISHOP KENNEDY ARGYLL

One of the few Scottish washed-rind cheeses, this is made by the Inverloch Cheese Company in Campbeltown. The curd is molded but not pressed, then brined and washed with a solution containing *Brevibacterium linens* as it matures. Matured for three months, the cheese develops a sticky orange rind over a pale yellow paste. The texture is soft and smooth, and the flavor is mild with a spicy note.

SIZE	
D. 9in (23cm)	
H. 1½in (4cm)	
WEIGHT	
3¾lb (1.7kg)	
SHAPE Round	
MILK Pasteurized cow's	
RENNET Vegetarian	
TYPE Modern	

BURWASH ROSE EAST SUSSEX

A washed-rind cheese made by the Traditional Cheese Dairy, Wadhurst, this cheese uses local unpasteurized cow's milk. A solution of *Brevibacterium linens* is added to the milk, and the cheese is matured for six to eight weeks, during which time it is washed with a brine solution containing rosewater. The resulting cheese has a ridged natural rind over a pale yellow paste with a moist texture and a mild, rich flavor.

SIZE	
D. 5½in (14cm)	
H. 2½in (6cm)	
WEIGHT	
1¾lb (800g)	
SHAPE Round	
MILK Unpasteurized cow's	
RENNET Vegetarian	
TYPE Modern	

CARK CUMBRIA

Martin Gott makes this cheese seasonally, during March to October, at Holker Farm Dairy using unpasteurized milk from the farm's goats. During the cheese-making, the rind of the cheese is washed, giving it the orange-brown rind that is characteristic of washed-rind cheeses. The paste inside is white, with a moist, crumbly texture and a salty flavor that has an element of goat to it.

SIZE
D. 8in (20cm)
H. 4in (10cm)
WEIGHT
6½lb (3kg)
SHAPE Round
MILK Unpasteurized goat's
RENNET Traditional animal
TYPE Modern

CAWS CERWYN PEMBROKESHIRE

Pant Mawr makes this unpressed cheese using cow's milk from the local cooperative. The curd is scalded, drained, molded, and salted, then matured unwrapped for three weeks. At this stage, the cheese has a pale apricot-colored rind, ridged from the mats on which it was drained, and is lightly dusted with white mold. The paste within is pale yellow with a moist texture and a mild, salty-sweet flavor.

SIZE
D. 6¾in (17cm)
H. 2in (5cm)
WEIGHT
2¾lb (1.2kg)
SHAPE Round
MILK Pasteurized cow's
RENNET Vegetarian
TYPE Modern

CELTIC PROMISE CEREDIGION

Made by John Savage of Teifi Farmhouse Cheese using raw cow's milk sourced from a single herd, this shaped cheese is matured for seven weeks in a humid atmosphere. During this time it is washed twice a week with a solution containing *Brevibacterium linens*, which acts on the cheese to create flavor and texture. It has a sticky orange rind, a pungent smell, a soft, giving texture, and a rich, full flavor.

SIZE	
D. 2¾in (7cm)	
H. 2in (5cm)	
WEIGHT	
1lb 2oz–1lb 5oz (500g–600g)	
SHAPE Round	
MILK Unpasteurized cow's	
RENNET Vegetarian	
TYPE Modern	

BUFFALO'S MILK

It may come as a surprise to discover that there is a handful of cheesemakers in Britain today creating buffalo's milk cheeses. The water buffalo, with its placid temperament, has long been valued for its milk in countries including Italy (famous for its buffalo mozzarella), India, and Pakistan.

Very low in carotene, buffalo's milk is a pure brilliant white and is naturally homogenous, with the small fat globules evenly distributed. Buffalo's milk contains 58 percent more calcium, 40 percent more protein, and higher levels of lactose than cow's milk, and some believe because of its greater concentration of solids, it is far more digestible. More curd can be obtained from buffalo's milk, hence making more cheese than the equivalent amount of cow's milk.

HEALTHY CHOICE
Buffalo's milk contains around 40per cent less cholesterol than cow's milk.

CRIFFEL DUMFRIES

This organic Scottish cheese is made by the Loch Arthur Community at Beeswing using milk from its biodynamic farm. Criffel is both a washed-curd and a washed-rind cheese, sprayed with a bacterial mixture containing *Brevibacterium linens* while it is ripened for a month. The cheese has a textured golden-orange rind and a smooth, shiny primrose yellow paste. Very flavorful, it is sweet with pleasant bitter notes.

SIZE	
D. 7in (18cm)	
H. 1½in (4cm)	
WEIGHT	
4lb (1.8kg)	
SHAPE Square	
MILK Unpasteurized organic cow's	
RENNET Vegetarian	
TYPE Modern	

CROFTON CUMBRIA

Thornby Moor Dairy, Thursby, makes this cheese—one of the few cheeses produced from a mixture of milks—using both locally sourced cow's milk and goat's milk. Matured for at least two weeks at the dairy, the cheese develops a natural rind over a pale paste. The texture is soft and moist, and the flavor of the cow's milk comes through first, followed by an aftertaste from the goat's milk.

SIZE	
D. 5½in (14cm)	
H. 1½ in (4cm)	
WEIGHT	
1lb 2oz (500g)	
SHAPE Domed round	
MILK Unpasteurized cow's and goat's	
RENNET Vegetarian	
TYPE Modern	

DODDINGTON BALTIC
NORTHUMBERLAND

This washed-rind cheese from Doddington Dairy uses unpasteurized milk from the farm's cows and traditional animal rennet. Once molded, the cheese is washed with Baltic Summer ale as it matures. It has a strong aroma, a golden-orange rind over a shiny pale yellow paste, and a long-lasting flavor with a sweet alcoholic note.

SIZE	
D. 7in (18cm)	
H. 1½in (4cm)	
WEIGHT	
4lb (1.8kg)	
SHAPE Round	
MILK Unpasteurized cow's	
RENNET Traditional animal	
TYPE Modern	

DRAGON'S BACK POWYS

Named after a peak in the Black Mountains, this Welsh cheese is made by Caws Mynydd Dhu on its farm at Brecon using sheep's milk from the farm's own Poll Dorset crosses. The curd is delicately handled during the making process, which involves milling and pressing. Matured for eight weeks in the cellar, it develops a pale natural rind and a creamy-textured paste that has a subtle flavor.

SIZE	
D. 4½in (11cm)	
H. 4in (10cm)	
WEIGHT	
2lb (900g)	
SHAPE Round	
MILK Pasteurized sheep's	
RENNET Vegetarian	
TYPE Modern	

DREWI SANT PEMBROKESHIRE

This small cheese is made by Pant Mawr using cow's milk brought in from a local cooperative. *Penicillium candidum* is added to the milk with the starter and the molded, unpressed curd is sprayed with honey mead before being wrapped and left to mature. The cheese is ready for eating at three weeks, by which time it has a faint dusting of white mold and a soft, pale yellow paste with a full flavor.

SIZE	
D. 4in (10cm)	
H. 2in (5cm)	
WEIGHT	
2lb–2½lb (900g–1.1kg)	
SHAPE Round	
MILK Pasteurized cow's	
RENNET Vegetarian	
TYPE Modern	

DURRUS CO CORK

This Irish cheese has been made by Durrus Farmhouse Cheese since 1979. The unpasteurized cow's milk is sourced locally and curdled with traditional animal rennet. A washed-rind cheese, it develops an orange-pink rind over a yellow paste; the small cheeses are matured for two weeks, and the large for four to five weeks. When young, the flavor is mild; as it matures, it becomes more complex with a fruity, nutty taste.

SIZE	
D. 4in (10cm) & 7in (18cm)	
H. 2in (5cm) & 2½in (6cm)	
WEIGHT	
13oz (380g) & 3lb 3oz (1.5kg)	
SHAPE Round	
MILK Unpasteurized cow's	
RENNET Traditional animal	
TYPE Modern	

GUBBEEN CO CORK

Gubeen Farmhouse has been making this cheese since 1979 using milk from its cows. The molded cheese is washed with white wine as it matures, to encourage the growth of the unique bacteria in the dairy that gives the cheese its particular flavor. Matured for between three weeks to six months, depending on size, the cheese has a pink-orange rind over a smooth yellow paste with a creamy, mushroomy flavor.

SIZE	
D. 4–12in (10–30cm)	
H. 2–4in (5–10cm)	
WEIGHT	
1lb 2oz–9lb (500g–4kg)	
SHAPE Round	
MILK Pasteurized cow's	
RENNET Vegetarian	
TYPE Modern	

IAMBORS SOMERSET

One of a handful of British buffalo's milk cheeses, this is made by Alham Wood Cheese in Shepton Mallet using organic milk from its own herd of buffalos. It is named after the Alham Wood's first buffalo bull. Iambors is covered with a coat of pale yellow wax, which protects the interior white paste. The texture is soft and crumbly, and the cheese has a mild lactic flavor.

SIZE	
D. 7in (18cm)	
H. 2½in (6cm)	
WEIGHT	
3lb 3oz–4½lb (1.5–2kg)	
SHAPE Round	
MILK Pasteurized buffalo's	
RENNET Vegetarian	
TYPE Modern	

IONA CROMAG ISLE OF MULL

Isle of Mull Cheeses at Sgriob-ruadh Farm Dairy, Tobermory, makes this cheese using unpasteurized sheep's milk. As the cheese matures, it is rind-washed with Iona whisky from the Tobermory distillery and a solution containing *Brevibacterium linens*. Ready to eat at a month, Iona Cromag has a sticky pale orange rind and a moist light-colored paste with a delicate buttery, mushroomy flavor.

SIZE	
D. 4½in (11cm) & 9in (23cm)	
H. 1½in (4cm)	
WEIGHT	
1lb 2oz (500g) & 5½lb (2.5kg)	
SHAPE Round	
MILK Unpasteurized sheep's	
RENNET Vegetarian	
TYPE Modern	

KEBBUCK DUMFRIES

This distinctive-looking semi-soft cheese is made by the Loch Arthur Community at Beeswing using organic milk from its herd of cows. The curd is washed at a high temperature, a fact reflected in the cheese's supple texture, and hung in a cloth to mature for two months. It has a ridged dark brown rind and a pale yellow paste with a rich salty-sweet fullness of flavor that lingers.

SIZE	
D. 4¾in (12cm)	
H. 2½in (6cm)	
WEIGHT	
1½–1¾lb (675–800g)	
SHAPE Varies	
MILK Unpasteurized cow's	
RENNET Vegetarian	
TYPE Modern	

KELTIC GOLD CORNWALL

This semi-soft cheese is made by Whalesborough Farm Foods in Bude. During the making process, the curd is washed, creating a particular supple texture. While the molded cheese is maturing, it is washed with local cider. It is ready to eat at six weeks, by which time it has a sticky apricot-colored rind and a shiny, moist pale yellow paste with a pungent smell. The taste is creamy and full.

SIZE	
D. 8in (20cm)	
H. 3in (7.5cm)	
WEIGHT	
3lb 3oz (1.5kg)	
SHAPE Round	
MILK Pasteurized cow's	
RENNET Vegetarian	
TYPE Modern	

KILLIECHRONAN ISLE OF MULL

This sheep's milk cheese is made by Isle of Mull Cheeses at Sgriob-ruadh Farm Dairy, Tobermory, using unpasteurized milk. During the making process, the curd is washed, brined, and pressed into a basket which gives the cheese its distinctive form. Matured for six months, it is an ivory-colored cheese with a moist, tender texture and a delicate flavor that has a long-lasting finish.

SIZE	
D. 2½in (6cm) & 3in (7.5cm)	
H. 6½in (16cm) & 9in (23cm)	
WEIGHT	
3lb 3oz (1.5kg) & 6½lb (3kg)	
SHAPE Oval	
MILK Unpasteurized sheep's	
RENNET Vegetarian	
TYPE Modern	

KNOCKDRINNA CO KILKENNY

This sheep's milk cheese is made by Knockdrinna Farmhouse Cheese, Stoneyford. The curd is washed, and while the cheese is matured for at least two months, the rind is washed with organic white wine, during which time it takes on a deep pink-orange color. The creamy-colored paste is dotted with a few holes and has a supple texture; the flavor is sweet and nutty with a long-lasting finish.

SIZE	
D. 9in (23cm)	
H. 3¼in (8cm)	
WEIGHT	
5½lb (2.5kg)	
SHAPE Round	
MILK Pasteurized sheep's	
RENNET Vegetarian	
TYPE Modern	

LAVISTOWN CO KILKENNY

Originally made by Olivia Goodwillie, a pioneer of the revival of Irish farmhouse cheese-making, Lavistown is now made by Knockdrinna Farmhouse Cheese. Using semi-skim milk, it is molded and pressed, with the rind washed in the early stages, and brushed as it matures. Ready to eat at four weeks, it has a moist yellow paste and fresh, creamy flavor. As it matures, it becomes drier and stronger-tasting.

SIZE	
D. 9in (23cm)	
H. 3½in (9cm)	
WEIGHT	
7½lb (3.5kg)	
SHAPE Round	
MILK Pasteurized cow's	
RENNET Vegetarian	
TYPE Modern	

LITTLE STINKY CORNWALL

This irreverently named washed-rind cheese is made for Country Cheeses by Sue Proudfoot at Whalesborough Farm near Bude. Using pasteurized cow's milk, it is washed with a brine and mold solution as it matures. Ready to eat at two to three months, it has a sticky orange-colored rind, while the paste is yellow with an almost meaty texture. As the name suggests, it has a distinctive smell and a mild, full flavor.

SIZE	
D. 3½in (9cm)	
H. 2in (5cm)	
WEIGHT	
14oz (400g)	
SHAPE Round	
MILK Pasteurized cow's	
RENNET Vegetarian	
TYPE Modern	

MILLEENS CO CORK

The Steeles have been making Milleens on the Beare Peninsula in the southwest of Ireland since 1976. Using pasteurized milk from a neighboring herd and animal rennet, this is a washed-rind cheese. The humid air in this part of Ireland encourages the growth of the molds, and the maturing process sees an orange-pink rind develop over a yellow paste which has a rich, complex flavor and creamy texture.

SIZE	
D. 4in (10cm) & 8in (20cm)	
H. 1¼in (3cm) & 1½in (4cm)	
WEIGHT	
8oz (225g) & 3lb (1.3kg)	
SHAPE Round	
MILK Pasteurized cow's	
RENNET Traditional animal	
TYPE Modern	

MISS MUFFET CORNWALL

Whalesborough Farm Foods, near Bude, makes this cow's milk semi-soft cheese. The curd is washed during the making process, giving it a supple texture. As the cheese matures, it develops a natural brown rind, which is flecked with white and pink mold. The resulting paste is smooth and pale yellow, and dotted with a few holes. The flavor is mild with a little zing at the end.

SIZE	
D. 3in (7.5cm) & 8in (20cm)	
H. 2in (5cm) & 4in (10cm)	
WEIGHT	
12oz (350g) & 3lb 3oz (1.5kg)	
SHAPE Round	
MILK Pasteurized cow's	
RENNET Vegetarian	
TYPE Modern	

MORN DEW SOMERSET

This cow's milk cheese is made at White Lake Cheeses, Bagborough Farm. During making, the curd is washed, creating a supple texture, and the rind is washed as the cheese matures, being ready to eat at between six to seven weeks. At this stage, Morn Dew has developed a sticky, thick orange-brown rind, while the paste is smooth and ivory-colored. The flavor is full with a sweet nuttiness and a slight tang.

SIZE	
D. 7in (18cm)	
H. 2½in (6cm)	
WEIGHT	
4lb (1.8kg)	
SHAPE Round	
MILK Pasteurized cow's	
RENNET Vegetarian	
TYPE Modern	

OXFORD ISIS OXFORDSHIRE

This small washed-rind cheese is made for the Oxford Cheese Company, which sells cheese in Oxford. During its maturation, the cow's milk cheese is washed with honey mead, affecting both its texture and its flavor. When Oxford Isis is ready to eat, it has a strong penetrating odor, a sticky pale orange rind, and a pale yellow paste with a supple, giving texture and a full, mushroomy flavor.

SIZE	
D. 4in (10cm)	
H. 1in (2.5cm)	
WEIGHT	
8oz (225g)	
SHAPE	Round
MILK	Pasteurized cow's
RENNET	Vegetarian
TYPE	Modern

POLMESK CORNWALL

Menallack Farm at Treverna, near Penryn, makes this goat cheese using Cornish goat's milk. The curd is molded, brined, allowed to dry, then, when it is around a week old, waxed to preserve the cheese. The resulting cheese has a dark green wax coating, while the paste inside is bright white. The texture is at once firm and moist, while the flavor is very mild, only slightly salty, and with the merest hint of goatiness.

SIZE	
D. 6¾in (17cm)	
H. 3in (7.5cm)	
WEIGHT	
1lb 2oz (500g)	
SHAPE	Round
MILK	Pasteurized goat's
RENNET	Vegetarian
TYPE	Modern

POSBURY DEVON

This flavored goat cheese is made by Norworthy Dairy, Crediton, using unpasteurized milk from its herd of Saanen, Toggenburg, and British Alpine goats. It is a washed-curd cheese, flavored with garlic, onion, horseradish, and paprika, and aged for a month. It has an orange rind over a springy white paste, dotted with holes and orange-red flecks. The flavor is mild with a faint spiciness to it.

SIZE	
D. 7in (18cm)	
H. 4½in (11cm)	
WEIGHT	
4½–5½lb (2–2.5kg)	
SHAPE Round	
MILK Pasteurized goat's	
RENNET Vegetarian	
TYPE Modern	

PUDDLE SOMERSET

This is made by White Lake Cheeses at Bagborough Farm using thermized milk (that is, heated for at least 15 seconds at a temperature between 135°F (57°C) and 154°F (68°C) from the farm's own goats. A mold-ripened cheese, it is aged for around six weeks, and develops a pale brown rind blotched with gray and white mold. The white paste has a smooth texture, while its flavor is sweet and nutty.

SIZE	
D. 4½in (11cm)	
H. ¾in (2cm)	
WEIGHT	
3½–5oz (100–140g)	
SHAPE Round	
MILK Thermized goat's	
RENNET Vegetarian	
TYPE Modern	

WASHED RINDS

Many semi-soft varieties, such as Celtic Promise (see page 79), are washed with a bacterial solution as they mature in order to create a sticky orange rind.

RACHEL SOMERSET

White Lake Cheeses at Bagborough Farm makes this cheese using milk from its own goats. The curd is washed, creating a supple texture, and the rind is also washed as the cheese matures, being ready to eat at between six to seven weeks. By this stage, the cheese has developed a sticky chestnut-colored rind and a smooth white paste. The flavor is mild with a nutty, subtle goatiness to it.

SIZE	
D. 7in (18cm)	
H. 2¾in (7cm)	
WEIGHT	
4½lb (2kg)	
SHAPE Round	
MILK Thermized goat's	
RENNET Vegetarian	
TYPE Modern	

RUBY GOLD YORKSHIRE

Cheesemongers Cryer & Stott have created this novelty cheese, inspired by the local Wakefield rhubarb triangle. A young, moist sheep's milk cheese is halved and layered with salted rhubarb, then matured for seven days. The cheese is sold at two weeks old and has a moist white paste, with a visible layer running through it. The clean, fresh flavor of the cheese contrasts with the sweetness of the rhubarb.

SIZE	
D. 2½in (6cm)	
H. 1¼in (3cm)	
WEIGHT	
1¾lb (800g)	
SHAPE Round	
MILK Pasteurized sheep's	
RENNET Vegetarian	
TYPE Modern	

SAVAL CEREDIGION

Made by Teifi Farmhouse Cheese, using raw milk sourced from a single herd, this shaped cheese is matured for seven to eight weeks in a humid atmosphere. During maturing, it is washed twice a week with a solution containing *Brevibacterium linens* that acts on the cheese to create flavor and texture. The resulting cheese has a sticky orange rind, a pungent smell, a soft, moist texture, and a rich, full flavor.

SIZE	
D. 10½in (26cm)	
H. 2in (5cm)	
WEIGHT	
4½lb (2kg)	
SHAPE Round	
MILK Unpasteurized cow's	
RENNET Vegetarian	
TYPE Modern	

SHARPHAM RUSTIC DEVON

This semi-soft cheese is made on the Sharpham Estate using unpasteurized milk from its Jersey cows. Unpressed, it is shaped in a colander and matured for six to eight weeks, during which time a pale natural rind, coated in white mold, forms over a rich yellow paste. The texture is creamy with a mild sweetness of flavor. Sharpham Rustic is also available flavored with chives and garlic.

SIZE	
D. 7in (18cm)	
H. 3½in (9cm)	
WEIGHT	
3¾lb (1.7kg)	
SHAPE Oval	
MILK Unpasteurized cow's	
RENNET Vegetarian	
TYPE Modern	

SLOE TAVEY SOMERSET

Easy to spot due to its distinctive romantic shape, this heart-shaped goat's milk cheese is made for Country Cheeses by cheesemaker Peter Humphries of White Lake Cheeses. During maturation, the cheese is washed with Plymouth sloe gin to add flavor. Matured for two to three months, Sloe Tavey has a sticky orange-red rind and a powerful, penetrating odor with a rich, full flavor to match.

SIZE	
D. 3½in (9cm)	
H. 1in (2.5cm)	
WEIGHT	
10½oz (300g)	
SHAPE Heart	
MILK Unpasteurized goat's	
RENNET Vegetarian	
TYPE Modern	

ST GILES EAST SUSSEX

High Weald Dairy at Tremains Farm makes this semi-soft organic cheese using milk from the farm's herd of cows and naming it after the local Norman church. The inspiration was the Port Salut style of cheese found in France. The cheese's distinctive orange rind gains its color from organic carrot juice. The pale yellow paste has a soft, moist texture, while the flavor is mild and creamy.

SIZE	
D. 9½in (24cm)	
H. 2¾–3¼in (7–8cm)	
WEIGHT	
6lb (2.7kg)	
SHAPE Round	
MILK Pasteurized organic cow's	
RENNET Vegetarian	
TYPE Modern	

ST JAMES CUMBRIA

Martin Gott makes this cheese at Holker Farm Dairy using unpasteurized milk from his own Lacaune sheep and animal rennet. It is named in tribute to the late pioneering cheesemaker and maturer James Aldridge, who taught Martin how to make cheese. St. James is washed with a brine solution as it matures, and has an orange rind over a firm, moist white paste with a nutty, salty flavor.

SIZE	
D. 8in (20cm)	
H. 1¾in (4.5cm)	
WEIGHT	
4lb (1.8kg)	
SHAPE Round	
MILK Unpasteurized sheep's	
RENNET Traditional animal	
TYPE Modern	

ST OSWALD WORCESTERSHIRE

This small organic cheese, named after a Worcestershire patron saint, is made by Gorsehill Abbey Farm using milk from its own herd of cows. A washed-rind cheese, it is matured for between one to three months, during which time the rind changes in color from yellow to a rich orange. The smooth pale yellow paste has a rich fullness of flavor and a long-lasting finish.

SIZE	
D. 4½in (11cm) & 13¾in (35cm)	
H. 1¾in (4.5cm)	
WEIGHT	
12oz (350g) & 5½lb (2.5kg)	
SHAPE Round	
MILK Pasteurized organic cow's	
RENNET Traditional animal	
TYPE Modern	

STINKING BISHOP
GLOUCESTERSHIRE

Created and made by Charles Martell at Hunts Court, the inspiration for this cheese comes from the Cistercian monks who once farmed locally. As it matures, the rind is washed with perry (it is named after a perry pear variety). With a textured golden-orange rind and smooth yellow paste, it has a powerful odor and rich, savory flavor.

SIZE	
D. 5in (13cm) & 8¼in (21cm)	
H. 1¾in (4.5cm) & 2in (5cm)	
WEIGHT	
1lb 2oz (500g) & 3lb 3oz (1.5kg)	
SHAPE Round	
MILK Pasteurized cow's	
RENNET Vegetarian	
TYPE Modern	

SUFFOLK GOLD SUFFOLK

Suffolk Farmhouse Cheeses near Cobham makes this cheese using the golden creamy milk from its herd of pedigree Guernsey cows. Lightly pressed, the cheese is matured for 10 weeks, developing a golden natural rind. The rich yellow paste is dotted with a few small holes and has a creamy texture and a mild sweetness of flavor, with the butteriness of the Guernsey cow's milk coming through.

SIZE	
D. 8in (20cm)	
H. 2in (5cm)	
WEIGHT	
6½lb (3kg)	
SHAPE Round	
MILK Pasteurized cow's	
RENNET Vegetarian	
TYPE Modern	

WHITE NANCY SOMERSET

This is a white mold-ripened semi-soft cheese, which is made by White Lake Cheeses at Bagborough Farm using milk from the farm's own herd of goats. The milk is thermized (that is, heated for at least 15 seconds at a temperature between 135°F (57°C) and 154°F (68°C) at the start of the cheese-making process. The resulting cheese has a moist, crumbly paste and a delicate lactic flavor.

SIZE	
D. 4½in (11cm)	
H. 2¾in (7cm)	
WEIGHT	
1lb 2oz (500g)	
SHAPE	Round
MILK	Thermized goat's
RENNET	Vegetarian
TYPE	Modern

WIGMORE BERKSHIRE

The Wigmores of Village Maid Cheese make their eponymous cheese at their creamery. The sheep's milk is thermized and *Penicillium candidum* is added to it while the curd is washed during the making process. As the cheese matures for between four to six weeks, it develops a coating of bloomy white mold over a pale paste inside. The soft paste has a creamy texture and a mild, nutty sweetness.

SIZE	
D. 4in (10cm) & 6¾in (17cm)	
H. 1½in (4cm)	
WEIGHT	
14oz (400g) & 1¾lb (800g)	
SHAPE	Round
MILK	Unpasteurized sheep's
RENNET	Vegetarian
TYPE	Modern

HARD CHEESES

These firm-textured cheeses are usually large and are matured
for several months. As is usual with cheeses, diversity is the norm,
and hard cheeses have a notable range of textures, from the exquisite
crumbliness of a Kirkham's Lancashire, to the dry firmness of cheeses
such as Montgomery's Cheddar or Gabriel.

ALLERDALE CUMBRIA

This hard goat cheese was the first to be made by Thornby Moor Dairy, Crofton Hall, Thursby, and it still makes it today. A hard-pressed cheese, Allerdale is matured for at least six weeks, developing a natural rind, although it is best eaten at between three to four months old. When young, the pale paste has a moist, crumbly texture and a sweet, nutty flavor; when older, the paste is drier and the flavor more complex.

SIZE	
D. 4in (10cm) & 5½in (14cm)	
H. 4in (10cm) & 5½in (14cm)	
WEIGHT	
2¼lb (1kg) & 5½lb (2.5kg)	
SHAPE	Truckle (barrel)
MILK	Unpasteurized goat's
RENNET	Vegetarian
TYPE	Modern

ASHDOWN FORESTERS
EAST SUSSEX

Named after Ashdown Forest in Sussex, this is made by High Weald Dairy at Tremains Farm using organic milk from its cows. The cheese is unpressed, taking its shape and textured golden natural rind from the basket in which it is formed. Matured for three months, it has a moist pale yellow paste and a mild, nutty sweetness of flavor.

SIZE	
D. 8½in (22cm)	
H. 2¾-3¼in (7-8cm)	
WEIGHT	
5lb (2.2kg)	
SHAPE	Basket
MILK	Pasteurized organic cow's
RENNET	Vegetarian
TYPE	Modern

BELSTONE DEVON

Curworthy Cheese at Stockbeare Farm, Okehampton, makes this cheese using milk from its own herd of Friesian cows and vegetarian rennet. The curd is cut, scalded, molded, and pressed, with the cheese then matured for at least three months, developing a natural rind dusted with white mold. The paste is a pale yellow color with a firm, smooth texture and a mild yet lingering flavor.

SIZE	
D. 5½in (14cm) & 7in (18cm)	
H. 2½in (6cm) & 3½in (9cm)	
WEIGHT	
2¼lb (1kg) & 5½lb (2.5kg)	
SHAPE Round	
MILK Pasteurized cow's	
RENNET Vegetarian	
TYPE Modern	

BELTANE CEREDIGION

This Welsh sheep's cheese made by Caws Celtica uses unpasteurized milk sourced from the maker's own flock of Friesland sheep. It is a curd-washed cheese, based on a Gouda recipe, in which the washed curds are molded and matured from 3–18 months, depending on size. Once matured, the cheese has a white, mold-dusted golden-brown natural rind and a dryish pale paste with a lingering nutty sweetness.

SIZE	
D. 3¼–10in (8–25cm)	
H. 2½–3½in (6–9cm)	
WEIGHT	
9oz–10lb (250g–4.5kg)	
SHAPE Round & wheel	
MILK Unpasteurized sheep's	
RENNET Vegetarian	
TYPE Modern	

BERKSWELL WEST MIDLANDS

Named after the village in which it is made, this hard cheese is made by the Berskwell Cheese Company at Ram Hall using milk from its own sheep. Matured for around four months, the cheese develops a hard golden-orange rind that is marked from the mold in which it was formed and blotched with mold. The cream-colored paste inside has a hard, dense texture and a full, complex sweet nuttiness to its flavor.

SIZE	
D. 8in (20cm)	
H. 3½in (9cm)	
WEIGHT	
5¼lb (2.4kg)	
SHAPE Flattened sphere	
MILK Unpasteurized sheep's	
RENNET Traditional animal & vegetarian	
TYPE Modern	

BERWICK EDGE NORTHUMBERLAND

This large hard cheese is made by Doddington Dairy, North Doddington Farm, Wooler, using unpasteurized milk from the farm's own herd of cows. Matured for around 10 months, it is a Gouda-style cheese, developing a brown rind over a shiny rich yellow paste dotted with a few small holes. Berwick Edge has a powerful, sweet flavor that lingers in the mouth.

SIZE	
D. 9in (23cm) & 12½in (32cm)	
H. 2¾in (7cm) & 4in (10cm)	
WEIGHT	
11lb (5kg) & 22lb (10kg)	
SHAPE Round	
MILK Unpasteurized cow's	
RENNET Traditional animal	
TYPE Modern	

MATURING CHEESES
Some of the best cheesemongers mature young cheeses themselves. This is known as *affinage* in France, where the practice is more common.

BIRDOSWALD CUMBRIA

Named after a nearby Roman fort on Hadrian's Wall, this organic cheese is made by Slack House Organic Farm. It is made from a Scottish Dunlop recipe, dating back to 1688, using milk from the farm's Ayrshire cows. The cheese is pressed, clothbound, and matured for up to six months, developing a golden rind that is dusted with mold over a rich yellow paste. The texture is firm and creamy, and the flavor is full.

SIZE	
D. 10in (25cm)	
H. 4in (10cm)	
WEIGHT	
20lb (9kg)	
SHAPE Cylinder	
MILK Unpasteurized organic cow's	
RENNET Vegetarian	
TYPE Modern	

BLARLIATH ROSS-SHIRE

This Scottish hard cheese is named after the farm in Tain where it is made by Highland Fine Cheeses. The curd is "Cheddared" during the making process and the molded cheese is double-wrapped in cloth and larded to keep the moisture in during the nine months' maturing time. As it matures, Blarliath develops a pale natural rind over a moist yellow paste that has a mild flavor.

SIZE	
D. 12in (30cm)	
H. 18in (46cm)	
WEIGHT	
40–48½lb (18–22kg)	
SHAPE Truckle	
MILK Pasteurized cow's	
RENNET Traditional animal	
TYPE Modern	

BUTTERCUP EAST SUSSEX

The Traditional Cheese Dairy in Wadhurst makes this cow's cheese using unpasteurized Jersey cow's milk, sourced from local dairies. The molded cheese is matured for three to four months, during which time it develops a ridged brown natural rind, dotted with white mold over a paste which is a rich yellow color, due to the Jersey cow's milk. The paste is firm and smooth, and the flavor is mild and creamy.

SIZE	
D. 7in (18cm)	
H. 3½in (9cm)	
WEIGHT	
7½lb (3.5kg)	
SHAPE	Cylinder
MILK	Unpasteurized cow's
RENNET	Vegetarian
TYPE	Modern

BUXLOW PAIGLE SUFFOLK

Farmhouse Fayre, Friston, makes this cheese using milk from its herd of Friesians. The picturesque name *paigle* is from the Suffolk dialect name for a cowslip. To make the cheese, the curd undergoes a process of cutting, salting, and pressing in molds. The molded cheese is waxed and matured for two months. Under the dark green wax coating, the pale yellow paste is moist with a mild lactic flavor.

SIZE	
D. 12in (30cm)	
H. 4¾in (12cm)	
WEIGHT	
11lb (5kg)	
SHAPE	Round
MILK	Pasteurized cow's
RENNET	Vegetarian
TYPE	Modern

CAERPHILLY

DYFED, CEREDIGION, & SOMERSET

A TRADITIONAL WELSH CHEESE, Caerphilly takes its name from
the town and county in South Wales where it was first made.
Like other hard cheeses, it was valued as an easily portable,
nourishing food, and by 1830, demand was such that a cheese market had been set
up to cater to it. It was said to be a favorite with Welsh coal miners, as its shallow
depth and thick rind made it easy to eat with dirty hands, while its moist, salty paste
helped replace the minerals and moisture lost by the miners through sweat.

CHANGING TIMES

The 19th century saw demand for Caerphilly exceed supply. The coming of the
railways led many Welsh farmers to export their milk for sale rather than use it to
make Caerphilly. To fill the gap, Somerset farmers, who traditionally made slow-
maturing Cheddar, began making their own Caerphilly cheese. During World War II,
the making of Caerphilly was banned by the Ministry of Food in favor of longer-lasting
hard cheeses. Even after the war, when the restriction had been lifted, very little
Caerphilly was made in Wales other than in large-scale creameries. Farmhouse
production, however, was continued in Somerset, notably by Duckett's Caerphilly
(see overleaf), and recent years have seen a revival in farmhouse Caerphilly.

Made from cow's milk, farmhouse Caerphilly is wheel-shaped, only lightly
pressed to retain moisture in the curd, and eaten young. A classic Caerphilly such as
Gorwydd has a pale paste with a noticeably flaky texture and a fresh, lemony flavor.

**GORWYDD
CAERPHILLY**

SIZE	
D. 6¾in (17cm) & 10in (25cm)	
H. 2¾in (7cm) & 3¼in (8cm)	
WEIGHT	
4½lb (2kg) & 7½–9lb (3.5–4kg)	
SHAPE Round	
MILK Unpasteurized cow's	
RENNET Traditional animal	
TYPE Traditional	

crumbly texture

creamy near rind

brown natural rind

GORWYDD CAERPHILLY

Gorwydd is made by the Trethowans in Ceredigion in the traditional way, using unpasteurized milk and animal rennet. Matured for two months, it has a brown natural rind and a pale yellow paste. Creamy near the rind and crumbly in the middle, the cheese has a fresh and lemony flavor.

CAWS CENARTH CAERPHILLY
DYFED

This organic Caerphilly is made by Caws Cenarth, using milk sourced from Ffosyficer Organic Farm, Pembrokeshire. The curd is cut, molded, brined to seal the cheese, and lightly pressed, then matured for four to five weeks, at which time it is a pale yellow cheese with a flaky, moist texture. It has a fresh lactic flavor with a touch of citrus.

SIZE	
D. 10in (25cm)	
H. 3¼in (8cm)	
WEIGHT	
9lb (4kg)	
SHAPE Round	
MILK Pasteurized organic cow's	
RENNET Vegetarian	
TYPE Traditional	

DUCKETT'S CAERPHILLY
SOMERSET

Duckett's has been making Caerphilly since 1928. It uses unpasteurized milk from the dairy's herd, animal rennet, and traditional pint starters. The curd is pressed briefly, salted, pressed, brined, and matured for seven weeks. It develops a textured brown rind over a primrose-colored paste with an open texture and a clean, citrusy flavor.

SIZE	
D. 10in (25cm)	
H. 3in (7.5cm)	
WEIGHT	
9lb (4kg)	
SHAPE Round	
MILK Unpasteurized cow's	
RENNET Traditional animal	
TYPE Traditional	

CAIRNSMORE DUMFRIES

This hard sheep's cheese is made by Galloway Farmhouse Cheeses in Sorbie using organic unpasteurized milk from the farm's own flock of sheep. The salted curd is pressed into molds, then halved, wrapped, and stored, maturing for six months. The resulting matured cheese has an ivory-colored paste with a smooth, dense texture and an initial sharp, salty flavor, which turns into a sweet sheepiness.

SIZE	
D. 7in (18cm)	
H. 9in (23cm)	
WEIGHT	
9lb (4kg)	
SHAPE Truckle	
MILK Unpasteurized sheep's	
RENNET Vegetarian	
TYPE Modern	

CAMPSCOTT DEVON

This organic cheese, made on Middle Campscott Farm, Ilfracombe, uses milk from the farm's sheep. Campscott is matured for two months, during which time it develops a gray-brown natural rind over a firm pale primrose yellow paste. The texture and flavor are creamier and sheepier when made in the winter, and drier and nuttier when made in the summer. It is also available flavored with cumin seeds.

SIZE	
D.4¼in (10.5cm) & 5½in (14cm)	
H. 4in (10cm) & 6in (15cm)	
WEIGHT	
2¼lb (1 kg) & 4½lb (2kg)	
SHAPE Cylinder	
MILK Pasteurized organic sheep's	
RENNET Vegetarian	
TYPE Modern	

CAMPSCOTT GOAT DEVON

Campscott Farm, Ifracombe, makes this organic hard cheese using unpasteurized milk from its own goats. The delicate curds are lightly pressed to mold them, and then the shaped cheese is brined and matured for one month. This pale cheese has a fresh, barely goaty flavor when it is made in the winter, and a drier paste with a subtle taste of goat when it is made in the summer.

SIZE	
D. 5½in (14cm) & 5in (13cm)	
H. 3¾in (9.5cm) & 5in (13cm)	
WEIGHT	
2lb 2oz (960g) & 4¼lb (1.9kg)	
SHAPE Cylinder	
MILK Unpasteurized organic goat's	
RENNET Vegetarian	
TYPE Modern	

COW'S MILK

Britain's best-known traditional cheeses—Cheddar, Stilton, and Cheshire—are all made from cow's milk. Cows have a long lactation period, and their rich, creamy milk, which has large fat globules that rise to the surface and a firm casein structure, lends itself to cheese-making.

The most common breed in Britain's dairy industry is the black-and-white Friesian–Holstein, popular because of its high milk yield. Other breeds valued by cheesemakers include the Scottish Ayrshire, the rare Gloucester, and the Jersey. The milk varies from breed to breed, but is also affected by what the cows eat, the season, and the stage of lactation. Summer milk, produced when the cows have grazed on lush, rich pastures, rather than silage, is particularly valued by cheesemakers.

JERSEY COWS

The milk from Jersey cows is noted for its rich golden-yellow color.

CAWS NANTYBWLA
CARMARTHENSHIRE

Caws Nantybwla makes this cheese from an old family recipe on its own farm using milk from its herd of pedigree Holsteins and Jerseys. It is a pressed cheese, matured for at least a month. It has a golden rind over a rich yellow paste. The texture is firm yet moist, and the flavor is full and tangy. This cheese is available in flavored versions.

SIZE	
D. 3in (7.5cm) & 3½in (9cm)	
H. 3in (7.5cm) & 9in (23cm)	
WEIGHT	
4½lb (2kg) & 10lb (4½kg)	
SHAPE Round	
MILK Pasteurized & unpasteurized cow's	
RENNET Vegetarian	
TYPE Modern	

CAWS Y GRAIG PEMBROKESHIRE

This goat cheese is made by Pant Mawr Cheese at Pant Mawr Farm using locally sourced goat's milk. An unpressed hard cheese that is matured for up to 12 weeks, it has a textured white rind and an ivory-colored paste with a dry but slightly crumbly texture. The flavor is mild and nutty with a faint goatiness to it. As the cheese matures, the flavor develops more of a pronounced goat tang.

SIZE	
D. 7in (18cm)	
H. 2in (5cm)	
WEIGHT	
2¾lb (1.25kg)	
SHAPE Round	
MILK Pasteurized goat's	
RENNET Vegetarian	
TYPE Modern	

CHEDDAR
SOMERSET & GLOUCESTERSHIRE

BRITAIN'S BEST-KNOWN CHEESE is named after the village of Cheddar, by Cheddar Gorge in Somerset. It is a cheese with a venerable history: Henry II is known to have ordered a substantial quantity in 1170AD. During the reign of Elizabeth I, Thomas Fuller described the cheeses made at Cheddar as the "best and biggest in England"; so rare and so expensive that they could be found only "at some great man's table." In the early 18th century, author Daniel Defoe wrote of visiting the village of Cheddar in his book, *Tour through the Whole of Great Britain*. He described how local dairy farmers pooled their milk to make one large cheese, of which Defoe wrote approvingly, "without all dispute, it is the best cheese that England affords, if not that the whole world affords." Throughout the 17th and 18th centuries, Cheddar cheese commanded premium prices and was seen as a luxury to be enjoyed by the wealthy.

CORPORATION CHEESES

Thanks to their size and the fact that Cheddar requires several months to mature, each cheese demands a considerable investment of resources. For generations, Cheddar was produced in the cooperative tradition observed by Defoe, with dairies pooling their milk supplies, and it consequently became known as a "corporation cheese." The 19th century saw two villages combining their resources to make a memorable Cheddar to celebrate Queen Victoria's wedding: it measured more than 9ft (3m) in diameter and weighed a staggering 1,250lb (567kg). Even "ordinary" Cheddars were an impressive size, weighing between 90–120lb (40–52kg).

MONTGOMERY'S CHEDDAR

SIZE	
D. 12½in (32cm)	
H. 10½in (26cm)	
WEIGHT	
53lb (24kg)	
SHAPE Round	
MILK Unpasteurized cow's	
RENNET Traditional animal	
TYPE Traditional	

deep yellow paste

natural rind

dry, flaky texture

MONTGOMERY'S CHEDDAR
The Montgomery family in Somerset makes this artisan
Cheddar using its own unpasteurized milk. The curd is
passed through a mill, molded, pressed, dipped in hot
water, bandaged in muslin, and matured for at least
11 months. The flaky paste has a rich, long-lasting flavor.

SPECIALIST TECHNIQUES

The defining attribute of Cheddar manufacture is the technique known as "Cheddaring." Slabs of cut curd are layered on top of each other and turned frequently so that any remaining whey is forced out under the weight, and the slabs become pliable. The slabs are then milled—cut into small pieces—before being salted and pressed in molds.

During the 19th century, the cheesemaker Joseph Harding (1805–1876) experimented with Cheddar-making at his farm at Marksbury, paying scrupulous attention to hygiene and charting the process by which the cheese was made in great detail, with particular attention to temperature control. Harding's dictum was: "Cheese is not made in the field, nor in the byre, nor even in the cow, it is made in the dairy." Harding was a key figure in the spreading of Cheddar-making knowledge and techniques, and was consulted by Scottish, Danish, and American cheesemakers.

Harding's invention of the cheese mill helped greatly to standardize Cheddar production. The cheese mill automates the tearing of the curd into small pieces, a process previously done by hand. The mill saves a great deal of time and requires less labor, as well as producing a better-textured cheese.

THE CHEDDAR NAME

Cheddar-making techniques have spread around the world, exported during the 19th and 20th century by emigrants from Britain to countries such as the United States and Canada. The 20th century saw Cheddar-making increasingly standardized and industrialized, both in Britain and abroad. The agricultural depression following World War I put many Cheddar dairies out of business, and, although Cheddar was one of the few cheeses permitted to be made commercially during World War II, farmhouse production dropped sharply with the rise of industrial dairies. In 1939, there were 333 farms in the Southwest making Cheddar; by 1948 this had fallen to 57. By 1974, this figure had fallen even further, with only 32 farms in the Southwest still producing the cheese. By the 1970s, most Cheddar was being produced from pasteurized milk in the rindless block form beloved of supermarkets.

With no legal protection for the name, "Cheddar" is widely made in countries around the globe, and in many forms only loosely related to the historic cheese. Even in Britain, the name Cheddar can legally be applied to both a mass-produced block cheese wrapped in plastic and a lovingly matured, clothbound cheese made by a farmer using unpasteurized milk from his or her own cows. Patrick Rance, the great crusader for the preservation of British cheese, described the situation with

DAYLESFORD CHEDDAR

GLOUCESTERSHIRE

This Cheddar is made in a traditional way by Daylesford Creamery using organic milk from the estate's herd of Friesians, and animal rennet. It is molded, pressed, bandaged in cloth, and matured for at least nine months, developing a brown natural rind. With a flaky yellow paste, it is sweet and nutty with a long-lasting caramel finish.

SIZE	
D. 10in (25cm)	
H. 16in (40cm)	
WEIGHT	
20lb (9kg)	
SHAPE Truckle	
MILK Unpasteurized organic cow's	
RENNET Vegetarian	
TYPE Traditional	

DITCHEAT HILL CHEDDAR

SOMERSET

Greens of Glastonbury makes this Cheddar using unpasteurized milk from its cows and a vegetarian rennet. The molded, pressed cheese is clothbound and matured for at least a year, during which time it develops a natural rind over a pale yellow paste. It has a creamy texture, a mild, slow-burning fullness of flavor, and a sweet finish.

SIZE	
D. 15in (38cm)	
H. 12in (30cm)	
WEIGHT	
55lb (25kg)	
SHAPE Truckle	
MILK Unpasteurized cow's	
RENNET Vegetarian	
TYPE Traditional	

characteristic eloquence: "Even our most generous original gift to humanity, Cheddar, is known to comparatively few people. Most meet it in name alone. What they eat is some hard-pressed rectangular substitute, often foreign, usually emasculated in character, and chilled into irredeemable immaturity."

Thankfully, traditional Cheddar-makers today are seeking ways to protect and define the quality of what they produce. A Protected Designation of Origin (PDO) has been given to a group of dairy farmers known as West Country Farmhouse Cheddar. This PDO stipulates that the cheese must be made from local herds reared and milked in Cornwall, Devon, Dorset, or Somerset; that it must contain no coloring, flavoring, or preservatives; that it must be made by traditional methods including "Cheddaring"; and that it must then be matured on the farm where it was made for at least nine months.

BRITAIN'S FAVORITE

Cheddar continues to be Britain's favorite cheese, popular not only for eating, but also for cooking, with sales of Cheddar dominating the market. In Britain today, many varieties of Cheddar are produced everywhere from small dairies to large commercial creameries. It is a sign of the cheese's enduring popularity that, ever since the British Cheese Awards (see page 185) were founded in 1994, the Cheddar cheese category has consistently seen the largest number of entries.

FARMHOUSE CHEDDARS

In the West Country, where Cheddar's roots lie, a handful of farmhouse cheese-makers continue to make traditional clothbound Cheddar using unpasteurized milk and animal rennet. Each cheese weighs around 50-60lb (22–27kg) and is matured for at least 11 months. Fascinatingly, although these Cheddar cheeses are produced using the same traditional methods, they are all recognizably different from each other in terms of texture and flavor—a tangible reminder of the variety that can be produced by expert cheese-making.

Three Cheddar-makers—Montgomery's (see page 112), Keen's (see opposite), and Westcombe Dairy (see opposite)—have been recognized by the Slow Food movement, an international campaign for the preservation of traditionally produced, high-quality food, which has awarded them a Presidium (a grant for developing and publicizing their product). A world away from the moist, mild curd of supermarket Cheddars, these magnificent farmhouse cheeses, with their complex, rich lingering flavors, are something to treasure.

KEEN'S CHEDDAR SOMERSET

One of the Artisan Somerset Cheesemakers recognized by Slow Food, Keen's makes its traditional Cheddar using unpasteurized milk from its own cows at Moorhayes Farm. A pint starter is used to sour the milk at the beginning of the process, and the clothbound cheese is matured for 12 months. The natural rind covers a dense, moist yellow paste that has a nuttiness of flavor and a tangy bite to it.

SIZE	
D. 13in (32.5cm)	
H. 13in (32.5cm)	
WEIGHT	
58lb (26kg)	
SHAPE Truckle	
MILK Unpasteurized cow's	
RENNET Traditional animal	
TYPE Traditional	

WESTCOMBE CHEDDAR
SOMERSET

A traditional cheddar made by Westcombe Dairy, an Artisan Somerset Cheesemaker recognized by Slow Food, using unpasteurized milk and a pint starter. The molded, pressed curd is clothbound and matured for 12–18 months, developing a natural rind. The firm yellow paste has a salty-sweet flavor with a tang to it.

SIZE	
D. 10in (25cm)	
H. 10in (25cm)	
WEIGHT	
53lb (24kg)	
SHAPE Truckle	
MILK Pasteurized cow's	
RENNET Traditional animal	
TYPE Traditional	

CHESHIRE SHROPSHIRE

MENTIONED IN THE DOMESDAY BOOK OF 1086AD, Cheshire is considered to be Britain's oldest named cheese. It is a hard-pressed cow's milk cheese associated with the Cheshire plain, which covers parts of Cheshire, Shropshire, and Clwyd. Cattle were grazed on the salty pastures, which were said to impart a particular flavor to the cows' milk and so to the cheese. Cheshire matures excellently, allowing it to travel well, and by the 17th century it was being shipped to London. In 1660, the diarist Samuel Pepys wrote: "Hawley brought a piece of his Cheshire cheese, and we were merry with it," and so well-known was the cheese that taverns in the capital were named after it. By the late 18th century, Cheshire cheese had become an important element of the county's economy, and cheese fairs were held in many Cheshire towns.

MASS PRODUCTION

Two world wars and agricultural depression, however, almost destroyed traditional Cheshire production. The industrialization of Cheshire cheese-making and the rise of supermarkets saw factory-produced, plastic-wrapped block Cheshire dominate. Unprotected by law, Cheshire is now made worldwide, and only a handful of English cheesemakers such as Appleby's now produces the traditional clothbound version.

Cheshire's natural color is pale cream, but "red" Cheshire, actually orange in color, is also made by coloring the paste with carrot juice or annatto. Traditional Cheshire had a period of "finishing off," which involved skewering the cheeses midway through maturation, renewing the cheesecloth, and leaving them to age. This process inevitably led to the rise of a blue version, and Blue Cheshire cheese is still made today.

APPLEBY'S CHESHIRE

SIZE	
D. 12in (30cm)	
H. 10½in (26cm)	
WEIGHT	
48½lb (22kg)	
SHAPE	Round
MILK	Unpasteurized cow's
RENNET	Vegetarian
TYPE	Traditional

"red" paste

natural rind

flaky texture

APPLEBY'S CHESHIRE

Appleby's Dairy of Hawkstone Abbey Farm in Shropshire
makes this cheese using milk from its own cows. The
molded, pressed cheeses are wrapped in calico and
matured for two to six months. It has a flaky, moist
texture and a gentle yet complex and lingering flavor.

CHEVINGTON NORTHUMBERLAND

The Northumberland Cheese Company at Blagdon makes this cheese using locally sourced Jersey cow's milk from Wheelbirks' Jersey herd at Stocksfield, the oldest Jersey herd in Northumberland. The cheese is matured for between 10–12 weeks, during which time it develops a knobbly brown natural rind, dotted with white mold, over a smooth yellow paste. The paste is moist, and the cheese has a mild, creamy flavor.

SIZE	
D. 8in (20cm)	
H. 2in (5cm)	
WEIGHT	
4½–5½lb (2–2.5kg)	
SHAPE Wheel	
MILK Pasteurized cow's	
RENNET Vegetarian	
TYPE Modern	

CHEVIOT NORTHUMBERLAND

Named after the Cheviot Hills, this cheese is made by the Northumberland Cheese Company, established by Mark Robertson in 1984, and now based at Blagdon. The dairy uses locally sourced milk, which can be traced back to individual farms. A pressed cheese, it is wrapped and matured for nine months. The resulting cheese has a pale yellow paste with a smooth, moist texture and a buttery flavor.

SIZE	
D. 8in (20cm)	
H. 2in (5cm)	
WEIGHT	
4½–5½lb (2–2½kg)	
SHAPE Wheel	
MILK Pasteurized cow's	
RENNET Vegetarian	
TYPE Modern	

CLOCHANDIGHTER
ABERDEENSHIRE

This hard cow's cheese is made by Devenick Dairy using pasteurized milk from its cows. The milk is curdled, drained, cut, milled, molded, and pressed, then set aside to mature for three months. As it matures, it develops a pale natural rind over the pale yellow paste. The texture is moist and crumbly, and it has a mild, fresh flavor.

SIZE	
D. 9½in (24cm)	
H. 4¾in (12cm)	
WEIGHT	
13lb (6kg)	
SHAPE	Round
MILK	Pasteurized cow's
RENNET	Vegetarian
TYPE	Modern

COOLEA CO CORK

Coolea Farmhouse Cheese at Macroom has been making this cheese since the late 1970s. The recipe is in the Gouda style, and involves washing the curd, heating it, molding, pressing, and salting it in brine. The cheese is matured for around six months, during which time it develops a smooth deep yellow rind over a firm yellow paste. The taste, initially salty and savory, has a rich caramel sweetness that lingers.

SIZE	
D. 10in (25cm) & 13¾in (35cm)	
H. 4in (10cm)	
WEIGHT	
10lb (4.5kg) & 18–20lb (8.5–9kg)	
SHAPE	Millstone
MILK	Pasteurized cow's
RENNET	Traditional animal
TYPE	Modern

COQUETDALE NORTHUMBERLAND

Mark Robertson of the Northumberland Cheese Company created this handmade cheese on the Blagdon Estate in South Northumberland. The milk comes from the estate's own herd of Red Poll and Friesian cows, with each batch fully traceable. A mold-ripened cheese with a natural rind, Coquetdale has a supple texture to its paste and a rich, complex flavor with a noticeably long fruity finish.

SIZE	
D. 12in (30cm)	
H. 4in (10cm)	
WEIGHT	
4½–5½lb (2–2.5kg)	
SHAPE Wheel	
MILK Pasteurized cow's	
RENNET Vegetarian	
TYPE Traditional	

CORNISH CRUMBLY CORNWALL

Whalesborough Farm Foods, near Bude, makes this cow's milk cheese, inspired, as the name suggests, by the crumbly Lancashire style of cheese. The molded curd is pressed under its own weight and matured for four weeks. During this time, the cheese develops a knobbly brown rind, blotched with different-colored molds, over a pale yellow paste. It is fine-grained and crumbly, with a mild and milky flavor.

SIZE	
D. 8in (20cm)	
H. 2½in (6cm)	
WEIGHT	
3lb 3oz (1.5kg)	
SHAPE Round	
MILK Pasteurized cow's	
RENNET Vegetarian	
TYPE Modern	

CORNISH YARG CORNWALL

With a strikingly patterned rind (due to being wrapped in nettle leaves), this Cornish cheese is handmade following a 17th-century recipe that was rediscovered and made by a couple called Gray. The cheese's West Country-sounding name is "Gray" spelled backward. Today, it is produced by Lynher Dairies in Cornwall using the dairy's own milk. It has a smooth paste and a mild, slightly mushroomy flavor.

SIZE	
D. 11in (28cm)	
H. 3½in (9cm)	
WEIGHT	
6½lb (3kg)	
SHAPE Wheel	
MILK Pasteurized cow's	
RENNET Vegetarian	
TYPE Modern	

COTHERSTONE DURHAM

A traditional Dales cheese, Cotherstone is handmade by Joan Cross at Quarry House Farm near Barnard Castle. There has long been a tradition in the Dales of keeping cows and making cheese from their milk, and Joan grew up watching her mother make cheese. Matured for one to three months, Cotherstone has a natural rind, with some white and blue molds on it, a creamy texture, and a rich, buttery flavor.

SIZE	
D. 3- 8½in (7.5–22cm)	
H. 3in (7.5cm)	
WEIGHT	
1lb 2oz–6½lb (500g–3kg)	
SHAPE Wheel	
MILK Pasteurized cow's	
RENNET Vegetarian	
TYPE Modern	

CROGLIN CUMBRIA

Thornby Moor Dairy at Crofton Hall, Thursby, makes this hard sheep cheese seasonally, using locally sourced sheep's milk between February and October. The cheese is matured for at least a month, and is sold at an older age as the season progresses. It develops a natural rind over a pale paste, with a delicate sweetness and nutty flavor when young, becoming drier and fuller in flavor as it ages.

SIZE	
D. 2in (5cm) & 3½in (9cm)	
H. 8in (20cm)	
WEIGHT	
9oz (250g) & 2¾lb (1.2kg)	
SHAPE	Curling stone
MILK	Unpasteurized sheep's
RENNET	Vegetarian
TYPE	Modern

CHEESE CHAMPION

Patrick Rance's Wells Stores at Streatley was a treasure house of superb cheeses. Generous with his considerable knowledge, Patrick Rance (1917-1999) was a kind man, widely respected and held in deep affection. Many farmhouse cheesemakers still remember the help he gave them. On hearing of Charles Martell's plan to revive Double Gloucester, for example, Patrick sent him a blank check, and there are many similar anecdotes telling of his help and generosity.

Patrick once said that "a slice of good cheese is never just a thing to eat. It is a slice of history." He wrote knowledgeably and from the heart about farmhouse cheeses, and became an eloquent and influential spokesman for the movement to preserve Britain's traditional cheese-making heritage.

PATRICK RANCE
Rance battled to save British farmhouse cheeses from extinction.

CROMAL INVERNESS

This organic cheese is made by Connage Highland Dairy at Milton of Connage farm. The dairy uses milk from its own organic dairy herd, made up mostly of Holstein–Friesian with Jersey crosses and Norwegian Reds. The curd is "Cheddared," and pressed and sold at four weeks, when it has a pale rind over a creamy yellow paste with a moist, crumbly texture and a very mild flavor.

SIZE
D. 10in (25cm) & 16in (40cm)
H. 3½in (9cm) & 5½in (14cm)
WEIGHT
10lb (4.5kg) & 31lb (14kg)
SHAPE Round
MILK Pasteurized organic cow's
RENNET Vegetarian
TYPE Modern

CUDDY'S CAVE NORTHUMBERLAND

Doddington Dairy on North Doddington Farm, Wooler, makes this hard cheese using unpasteurized cow's milk from its own herd of cows, and traditional animal rennet. Made in the Dales style, the cheese is matured for between two to five months, during which time it develops a brown natural rind. The pale yellow paste has a smooth texture, and the cheese has a mild, nutty flavor with a long finish.

SIZE
D. 9in (23cm)
H. 2½in (6cm)
WEIGHT
9lb (4kg)
SHAPE Round
MILK Unpasteurized cow's
RENNET Traditional animal
TYPE Modern

CUMBERLAND FARMHOUSE

CUMBRIA

Thornby Moor Dairy, Thursby, makes this cheese using locally sourced unpasteurized cow's milk. The molded, pressed curd is clothbound and matured for at least two months, although it is at its best at five months. Under the natural rind, the pale yellow paste has a smooth texture and a rounded flavor, developing as the cheese matures.

SIZE	
D. 4–9in (10–23cm)	
H. 4–8in (10–20cm)	
WEIGHT	
2¼–20lb (1–9kg)	
SHAPE Truckle	
MILK Unpasteurized cow's	
RENNET Vegetarian	
TYPE Modern	

CURWORTHY DEVON

Based on an old 17th-century recipe, Curworthy is handmade by Rachel Stevens on her farm in Devon using milk from her herd of Holstein–Friesians. Depending on the size of the cheese, Curworthy is matured for between two to four months. It develops a natural rind, but is also available coated in black wax (as shown here). It is a low-acid cheese with a supple texture and a long-lasting buttery flavor.

SIZE	
D. 3½–8in (9cm–20cm)	
H. 2½in–4in (6cm–10cm)	
WEIGHT	
1–5lb (450g–2.2kg)	
SHAPE Cylinder	
MILK Pasteurized cow's	
RENNET Traditional animal	
TYPE Traditional	

DEESIDER ABERDEENSHIRE

Devenick Dairy in Banchory-Devenick, near Aberdeen, makes this cheese using pasteurized milk from the dairy farm's own herd of cows. The milk is curdled, drained, molded, and pressed, then the cheese is coated in green wax to protect it and retain moisture. Set aside to mature for six months, it develops a moist but firm pale yellow paste inside the wax coating and has a mild flavor.

SIZE	
D. 4¾in (12cm)	
H. 1¼in (3.5cm)	
WEIGHT	
3lb (1.3kg)	
SHAPE Wheel	
MILK Pasteurized cow's	
RENNET Vegetarian	
TYPE Modern	

DELAMERE DISTINCTIVE
CHESHIRE

Delamere Dairy makes this mature goat cheese using goat's milk sourced from various UK suppliers. A hard-pressed cheese, it is made in a large round, pressed for 18 hours, and matured for 9–12 months. The paste is ivory with a moist, crumbly texture, while the flavor is light but distinctly goaty with a nuttiness to the taste.

SIZE	
D. 13¾in (35cm)	
H. 5½in (14cm)	
WEIGHT	
31lb (14kg)	
SHAPE Round	
MILK Pasteurized goat's	
RENNET Vegetarian	
TYPE Modern	

DERBY SAGE WEST MIDLANDS

Fowlers of Earlswood have been making Derby cheese since 1840. They make this cheese from pasteurized cow's milk using a recipe that is more than 100 years old. As the milled curd is placed in the molds, a layer of chopped sage is added, giving the cheese a characteristic band of dark green flecks. The cheese has a firm, moist yellow paste, with the sage adding an herbal note to the creamy taste of the cheese.

SIZE	
D. 8in (20cm)	
H. 4in (10cm)	
WEIGHT	
3lb 3oz (1.5kg)	
SHAPE	Half-moon
MILK	Pasteurized cow's
RENNET	Vegetarian
TYPE	Traditional

DESMOND CO CORK

This Swiss-style cheese is made by the West Cork Natural Cheese Company. It is made only during the summer months, using milk from the Newmarket Cooperative. It is a thermophilic cheese (as are Gruyère and Emmental) made with a yogurt-like starter and matured for at least a year. Under the natural rind, the rich golden paste is firm and dry with a powerful, long-lingering flavor.

SIZE	
D. 12½in (32cm)	
H. 4–5in (10–13cm)	
WEIGHT	
15½lb (7kg)	
SHAPE	Round
MILK	Unpasteurized cow's
RENNET	Traditional animal & vegetarian
TYPE	Modern

DEVON OKE DEVON

Curworthy Cheese at Stockbeare Farm makes this cheese using unpasteurized cow's milk from the farm's own herd of Friesians, and uses animal rennet to curdle the milk. The curd is scalded, cut, molded, bathed in brine, and matured for at least three months. During maturation, the cheese develops a golden natural rind, dusted with white mold, over a smooth pale yellow paste which has a full, well-rounded flavor.

SIZE
D. 5½–8in (14–20cm)
H. 2½–5in (6–13cm)
WEIGHT
2¼–10lb (1–4.5kg)
SHAPE Round
MILK Pasteurized cow's
RENNET Traditional animal
TYPE Modern

DEVON SAGE DEVON

This flavored cheese is made for Country Cheeses by Rachel Stephens using milk from her Friesians. Chopped sage is added at the beginning of the cheese-making process with the curd, then molded, pressed, and brined. Matured for three to four months, the paste is moist and yellow inside a green wax coating. It is flecked with green from the sage, with the cheese both smelling and tasting of the herb.

SIZE
D. 7½in (19.5cm)
H. 3in (7.5cm)
WEIGHT
5lb (2.25kg)
SHAPE Round
MILK Pasteurized cow's
RENNET Vegetarian
TYPE Modern

DODDINGTON NORTHUMBERLAND

This Northumbrian hard cheese is made by Doddington Dairy, North Doddington Farm, Wooler. The dairy uses unpasteurized milk from the farm's cows and traditional animal rennet, and matures the cheese for 12–14 months. Doddington has a dark reddish-brown natural rind and a dry deep yellow paste with a faintly crystalline texture. The flavor is rich and salty-sweet with a long finish.

SIZE	
D. 9in (23cm) & 12½in (32cm)	
H. 4½in (11cm)	
WEIGHT	
11lb (5kg) & 22lb (10kg)	
SHAPE Round	
MILK Unpasteurized cow's	
RENNET Traditional animal	
TYPE Modern	

DOUBLE BERKELEY
GLOUCESTERSHIRE

Charles Martell revived the making of this cheese (documented in 1796 as being made in the Berkeley district of Gloucestershire). Annatto is added to create the distinctive mottled orange-and-white paste. The curd is molded, pressed, and matured for two to three months. It has a natural rind, a creamy texture, and a mild, sweet flavor.

SIZE	
D. 8½in (22cm)	
H. 2¾in (7cm)	
WEIGHT	
5lb (2.25kg)	
SHAPE Round	
MILK Pasteurized cow's	
RENNET Vegetarian	
TYPE Traditional	

DOUBLE GLOUCESTER
GLOUCESTERSHIRE & SHROPSHIRE

THE FERTILE COUNTY OF GLOUCESTERSHIRE is associated with Single
and Double Gloucester cheeses. Historically, these were made using
milk from Gloucester cattle, a handsome horned brown-black animal
with a distinctive white stripe down its back and along its belly. The Gloucester
was, and still is, valued for its gentle temperament and for producing good beef
and milk—the latter, with its small fat globules, is ideal for cheese-making.

SINGLE AND DOUBLE GLOUCESTER

The distinction between the two cheeses arose at the end of the 18th century:
Double Gloucester was exported outside the county, with cheese merchants touring
local farms to check the quality of their produce, while Single was reserved for
consumption at home. Double Gloucester is a bigger, thicker cheese than Single,
which may be where the names originated.

    The naming may also derive from the milk that makes up the cheeses. Single
Gloucester has a lower fat content than Double Gloucester, being partially made with
skim milk. Double Gloucester is richer, made from either the whole milk of two milkings
or with milk and additional cream. Double Gloucester is an older, harder cheese, with
annatto (an orange plant extract) added to produce the characteristic pale tangerine
color. In 1783 William Marshall, in his *Rural Economy of Gloucestershire*, described in
detail the making of Gloucester cheese. He described cheeses being piled two or four
high as they matured, with the rind already tough enough at one month for them to
be "thrown about like old cheeses." As a notoriously tough-rinded, hard-pressed

APPLEBY'S DOUBLE GLOUCESTER

SIZE	
D. 12½in (32cm)	
H. 6in (15cm)	
WEIGHT	
28½ lb (13kg)	
SHAPE	Round
MILK	Unpasteurized cow's
RENNET	Vegetarian
TYPE	Traditional

orange paste

smooth, firm texture

natural rind

DOUBLE WORCESTER
WORCESTERSHIRE

The county of Worcestershire's equivalent to a Double Gloucester, this is made by Ansteys at Broomhall Farm. Annatto is added to give it the distinctive orange color. The curd is double-cut and double-milled to give a finer texture. Matured for six months, it has a natural rind over a smooth, firm paste and a subtle fullness of flavor.

SIZE	
D. 8in (20cm)	
H. 6in (15cm)	
WEIGHT	
7½lb (3.5kg)	
SHAPE Round	
MILK Pasteurized cow's	
RENNET Vegetarian	
TYPE Modern	

DRUMLIN CO CAVAN

Corleggy Cheese makes this Irish cheese using unpasteurized cow's milk from a local farmer. The name comes from the drumlin pastures surrounding Corleggy on which the cows graze. Matured for at least six weeks, Drumlin develops a knobbly golden-brown rind over a firm, moist yellow paste with a rich, savory flavor. It is also available smoked and flavored with garlic and red pepper, cumin seeds, and peppercorns.

SIZE	
D. 3¼in (8cm) & 6½in (16cm)	
H. 2¾in (7cm) & 17½in (45cm)	
WEIGHT	
12oz (350g) & 2lb (900g)	
SHAPE Cylinder & round	
MILK Unpasteurized cow's	
RENNET Vegetarian	
TYPE Modern	

DRUMLOCH WHEEL ARGYLL

Inverloch Cheese makes this hard cow cheese at its creamery at Campbeltown, the Mull of Kintyre. It is made with Guernsey cow's milk from a herd grazed on the shores of West Loch Tarbet which, in the summer months especially, produces a rich yellow milk. The molded, pressed cheese is coated in green wax and matured for a year. Under the wax, the firm yellow paste has a creamy texture and a buttery savoriness.

SIZE	
D. 6in (15cm)	
H. 6in (15cm)	
WEIGHT	
6½lb (3kg)	
SHAPE Cylinder	
MILK Pasteurized cow's	
RENNET Vegetarian	
TYPE Modern	

DUDDLESWELL WEST SUSSEX

High Weald Dairy at Tremains Farm in Horsted Keynes makes this cheese using sheep's milk sourced from dedicated farms. Inspired by the tradition of the Dales cheeses and made by farmhouses as a way of storing milk, the cheese is matured for three months, developing a natural golden rind over a pale cream-colored paste. The texture is smooth and creamy, while the flavor has a mild, nutty sweetness.

SIZE	
D. 9½in (24cm)	
H. 2¾–3¼in (7–8cm)	
WEIGHT	
7lb (3.2kg)	
SHAPE Wheel	
MILK Pasteurized sheep's	
RENNET Vegetarian	
TYPE Modern	

DUNLOP AYRSHIRE

Dunlop, Scotland's indigenous hard cheese, was first made in the late 17th century. This variety is made by Ann Dorward at Dunlop Dairy at West Clerkland Farm, Stewarton, who first revived this traditional cheese using the rich milk from the farm's own Ayrshire cows. Matured for six months, it develops a pale primrose yellow paste with a firm, moist texture. The flavor is full with a lingering salty-sweetness to it.

SIZE	
D. 1½–12in (4–30cm)	
H. 2½–12in (6–30cm)	
WEIGHT	
14oz–44lb (400g–20kg)	
SHAPE Round	
MILK Pasteurized cow's	
RENNET Vegetarian	
TYPE Traditional	

DUTCHMAN WEST SUSSEX

This impressive-sized cheese is made on the biodynamic Old Plaw Hatch Farm using unpasteurized milk from the farm's cows, but only when they are producing enough. As the name suggests, this Gouda-style cheese is the legacy of a Dutch cheesemaker. Matured for three months, it develops a golden natural rind and a pale mild-tasting paste, and is available plain or flavored with cumin or peppercorns.

SIZE	
D. 13¾in (35cm) & 17in (43cm)	
H. 3¼in (8cm) & 4in (10cm)	
WEIGHT	
20lb (9kg) & 40lb (18kg)	
SHAPE Wheel	
MILK Unpasteurized cow's	
RENNET Vegetarian	
TYPE Modern	

ELGAR MATURE WORCESTERSHIRE

This hard clothbound cheese is made by Lightwood Cheese using unpasteurized cow's milk. The curd is molded in cloth-lined molds, pressed, dipped in hot water, then pressed again, dried, and matured for 9–12 months. It has a golden-brown rind, flecked with white and orange molds, and a deep yellow paste. The texture is firm but creamy, and the flavor is mellow with a touch of old-fashioned sharpness.

SIZE	
D. 8in (20cm)	
H. 5in (13cm)	
WEIGHT	
8½lb (3.8kg)	
SHAPE Circular truckle	
MILK Unpasteurized cow's	
RENNET Vegetarian	
TYPE Modern	

FOSSEWAY FLEECE SOMERSET

Made by the Somerset Cheese Company at Ditcheat Hill Farm, this hard sheep cheese is named after the local Fosseway. The curds are molded, pressed overnight, and matured for between 4–12 months, during which time the cheese develops a natural brown rind that is splotched with white mold. The pale creamy-white paste has a smooth, firm, waxy texture and a mild but lasting nutty flavor.

SIZE	
D. 7in (18cm) & 10in (25cm)	
H. 3in (7.5cm)	
WEIGHT	
4½lb (2kg) & 7½lb (3.5kg)	
SHAPE Wheel	
MILK Pasteurized sheep's	
RENNET Vegetarian	
TYPE Modern	

GABRIEL CO CORK

One of a handful of Swiss-style "thermophilic" cheeses made in Ireland and Britain, this variety is made by the West Cork Natural Cheese Company only during the summer. It uses a yogurt-like starter and milk from the Newmarket Cooperative, where the cheese is made. Matured for at least a year, it develops a natural rind and a hard, dry paste with a granular texture and a slow-burning, powerful fruity flavor.

SIZE	
D. 12½in (32cm)	
H. 4–4¾in (10–12cm)	
WEIGHT	
15½lb (7kg)	
SHAPE Round	
MILK Unpasteurized cow's	
RENNET Traditional animal & vegetarian	
TYPE Modern	

GALLYBAGGER ISLE OF WIGHT

Created and made by Isle of Wight Cheese, this cheese draws its name from a local dialect word for "scarecrow." Cheesemaker Richard Hodgson uses an Italian starter culture added to unpasteurized Guernsey cow's milk. The pressed cheese is matured for seven months, during which time it develops a dark brown natural rind over a rich yellow paste. The cheese has a long-lasting full, sweet, nutty flavor.

SIZE	
D. 10in (25cm)	
H. 5in (13cm)	
WEIGHT	
11lb (5kg)	
SHAPE Round	
MILK Unpasteurized cow's	
RENNET Vegetarian	
TYPE Modern	

GLEBE BRETHAN CO LOUTH

This impressive Gruyère-type cheese is made at the Tiernan Family Farm using unpasteurized milk from the farm's Montbeliarde herd and animal rennet. The large cheeses are matured on spruce wood for 6–18 months. During maturation, the cheese forms a natural brown rind over a dense, smooth yellow paste. Depending on age, the flavor ranges from fruity and buttery to a fuller, spicier taste when mature.

SIZE	
D. 26in (66cm)	
H. 4in (10cm)	
WEIGHT	
99lb (45kg)	
SHAPE Wheel	
MILK Unpasteurized cow's	
RENNET Traditional animal	
TYPE Modern	

GODMINSTER SOMERSET

This organic Cheddar is made for Godminster Farm using pasteurized organic cow's milk. The curd is "Cheddared," and the cheese is made in 44lb (20kg) blocks, which are matured for 12 months, then remilled and formed into assorted shapes and sizes and coated in Soil Association-certified burgundy-colored wax. Under the wax coating, the pale yellow paste has a fine-grained, moist texture and a salty-sweet flavor.

SIZE	
D. 3–6¼in (7.5–15.5cm)	
H. 1¾–4in (4.5–10cm)	
WEIGHT	
14oz–4½lb (400g–2kg)	
SHAPE Round & heart	
MILK Pasteurized organic cow's	
RENNET Vegetarian	
TYPE Traditional	

GRANITE CITY ABERDEENSHIRE

Devenick Dairy in Banchory-Devenick, near Aberdeen, makes this distinctive-looking cheese using pasteurized milk from the dairy farm's own herd of cows. The milk is curdled, drained, molded, and pressed. The cheese is then coated in green and red wax and set aside to mature for six months. The pale yellow paste inside the wax coating is moist and firm, and has a mild, creamy flavor.

SIZE	
D. 4¾in (12cm)	
H. 2in (5cm)	
WEIGHT	
1¼lb (550g)	
SHAPE	Wheel
MILK	Pasteurized cow's
RENNET	Vegetarian
TYPE	Modern

GUNSTONE GOAT DEVON

Norsworthy Dairy in Crediton makes this goat cheese using unpasteurized milk from its own herd of Saanen, Toggenburg, and British Alpine goats. Annatto is added to the milk to give the cheese its pale apricot-colored paste. The curd is washed, and the cheese is matured for two months, developing a natural golden rind. It has a moist paste and a mild, full, sweet flavor with a touch of goat.

SIZE	
D. 7in (18cm)	
H. 4½in (11cm)	
WEIGHT	
4½–5½lb (2–2.5kg)	
SHAPE	Round
MILK	Unpasteurized goat's
RENNET	Vegetarian
TYPE	Modern

HAMPSHIRE ROSE WILTSHIRE

This hard cheese is made by Loosehanger Farmhouse Cheeses at Home Farm, Salisbury. It is produced using Ayrshire milk from a single herd, which Loosehanger pasteurizes during the winter months, but not during the summer when the milk is at its rich best. Matured for at least six months, it has a golden rind and a firm ivory-colored paste. The flavor is full and salty-sweet with a lingering sweet finish.

SIZE	
D. 7½in (19.5cm)	
H. 4–4½in (10–11cm)	
WEIGHT	
7½–9lb (3.5–4kg)	
SHAPE Wheel	
MILK Seasonally unpasteurized	
RENNET Vegetarian	
TYPE Modern	

HAREFIELD GLOUCESTERSHIRE

Diana Smart at Old Ley Farm, noted for her Gloucester cheeses, also makes this hard cow's milk cheese using a mixture of skim and whole milk. The scalded curd is milled, dry-salted by hand, molded, and pressed. It is then matured for two years, during which time the cheese develops a craggy-textured brown rind over a dull yellow paste. The texture is hard and dry, and the flavor is powerful with a distinct tang.

SIZE	
D. 10in (25cm)	
H. 2in (5cm)	
WEIGHT	
5lb (2.2kg)	
SHAPE Wheel	
MILK Unpasteurized cow's	
RENNET Vegetarian	
TYPE Modern	

HAWKSTON SUFFOLK

Rodwell Farm Dairy, Baylham, makes this cheese using unpasteurized milk from Holstein-Friesians. The milk is ripened and curdled, then chopped, scalded, cut, and turned. It is placed in cloth-lined molds and pressed, muslin-bandaged, and matured for two to three weeks. The matured cheese has a natural brown rind, blotched with white mold, and a firm, pale yellow paste with a mild, lemony flavor.

SIZE	
D. 10in (25cm)	
H. 4in (10cm)	
WEIGHT	
9½–11lb (4.3–5kg)	
SHAPE	Wheel
MILK	Unpasteurized cow's
RENNET	Vegetarian
TYPE	Modern

HEREFORD HOP GLOUCESTERSHIRE

Created and made by Charles Martell at Dymock, close to the Herefordshire border, this cheese has a distinctive appearance due to the layer of toasted hops that encrust it. Made with whole pasteurized milk, it is molded, coated with hops, and matured for three months. The resulting cheese has a firm pale paste with a mild flavor, contrasting with the texture and ale note from the hops.

SIZE	
D. 8½in (22cm)	
H. 2¾in (7cm)	
WEIGHT	
5lb (2.25kg)	
SHAPE	Wheel
MILK	Pasteurized cow's
RENNET	Vegetarian
TYPE	Modern

INVERLOCH ARGYLL

This goat cheese is made by Inverloch Cheese at its creamery at Campbeltown, the Mull of Kintyre. Locally sourced goat's milk is used to make the cheese, which is made only during the months when the goats are in milk. The molded cheese is pressed and matured for four to six months, then coated in red wax. The white paste is firm and smooth, and it has a nutty sweetness without being overwhelmingly goaty.

SIZE	
D. 6in (15cm)	
H. 6in (15cm)	
WEIGHT	
6½lb (3kg)	
SHAPE Wheel	
MILK Pasteurized goat's	
RENNET Vegetarian	
TYPE Modern	

ISLE OF MULL ISLE OF MULL

This hard cheese is made by Isle of Mull Cheeses at Sgriob-Ruadh Farm Dairy, Tobermory, using unpasteurized milk from the farm's closed herd of cows and traditional animal rennet. The curd is milled, salted, molded, and pressed, then cloth-wrapped and matured in the cellar for six months. It has a textured brown natural rind over a yellow paste, and a powerful, complex, lingering flavor.

SIZE	
D. 2–11in (5–28cm)	
H. 3½–9in (9–23cm)	
WEIGHT	
14oz–55lb (400g–25kg)	
SHAPE Truckle & cylinder	
MILK Unpasteurized cow's	
RENNET Traditional animal	
TYPE Modern	

THICK SKINS

Hard cheeses such as this Berkswell (see page 102) often develop thick, tough rinds, which take their shape and texture from the containers in which they are molded.

JUNAS SOMERSET

Alham Wood in West Cranmore makes this organic cheese on its farm, using unpasteurized milk from its own herd of water buffalo. Junas is, in fact, named after the matriarch of the herd. The cheese is matured for four to eight months and has a pale brown rind, which is textured and blotched. The ivory paste inside has a dense, moist texture and a lactic flavor with a salty-sweetness to it.

SIZE	
D. 7in (18cm)	
H. 4in (10cm)	
WEIGHT	
2–2½lb (900g–1.1kg)	
SHAPE Round	
MILK Unpasteurized organic buffalo's	
RENNET Vegetarian	
TYPE Modern	

KELSAE ROXBURGHSHIRE

This Scottish hard cheese is made by Stichill Jerseys, at Garden Cottage Farm, using unpasteurized milk from the farm's Jersey cows. The milk is coagulated, then the curd is cut, milled, dry-salted, placed in cheesecloth-lined molds, and pressed for seven days before being wrapped and matured for four to six months. The matured cheese has a pale yellow paste with a moist, crumbly texture and mild, creamy flavor.

SIZE	
D. 8in (20cm)	
H. 8in (20cm)	
WEIGHT	
9lb (4kg)	
SHAPE Wheel	
MILK Unpasteurized cow's	
RENNET Vegetarian	
TYPE Modern	

KIELDER NORTHUMBERLAND

Made by the Northumberland Cheese Company at Blagdon, this cheese is named after Kielder Forest. It is made from locally sourced Jersey cow's milk from Wheelbirks' Jersey herd at Stocksfield, the oldest Jersey herd in Northumberland. A young unpressed cheese, Kielder is matured for six weeks. At this age, the cheese has a pale yellow paste with a smooth, moist texture and a mild flavor.

SIZE	
D. 8in (20cm)	
H. 2in (5cm)	
WEIGHT	
4½–5½lb (2–2.5kg)	
SHAPE Wheel	
MILK Pasteurized cow's	
RENNET Vegetarian	
TYPE Modern	

KILLEEN COW CO GALWAY

Killeen Farmhouse Cheeses at Killeen Millhouse, Balllinasloe, makes this Irish cheese using milk from a neighbor's herd of cows. The cheese is made following a Gouda-style recipe, with the curd being washed, then molded and pressed. It is ready to eat at 10 weeks. A 10-week-old cheese has a creamy texture and mild flavor, whereas at 10 months the texture is drier and the flavor is fuller, although still sweet.

SIZE	
D. 12in (30cm)	
H. 4in (10cm)	
WEIGHT	
11lb (5kg)	
SHAPE Round	
MILK Pasteurized cow's	
RENNET Traditional animal	
TYPE Modern	

KILLEEN GOAT CO GALWAY

This Irish goat cheese is made by Killeen Farmhouse Cheeses, Ballinasloe, using milk from its goats. The cheese is made following a Gouda-style recipe, with the curd washed, then molded, pressed, and matured for at least eight weeks, developing a golden-brown natural rind. At this age, the white paste has a creamy texture and a sweetness; at 10 months, the texture is drier, with a more complex flavor.

SIZE	
D. 12in (30cm)	
H. 4in (10cm)	
WEIGHT	
11lb (5kg)	
SHAPE Round	
MILK Pasteurized cow's	
RENNET Vegetarian	
TYPE Modern	

KNOCKANORE CO WATERFORD

This is made by Knockanore Irish Farmhouse Cheese using unpasteurized milk from its Friesian cows. Once formed, the hard-pressed cheese is matured for at least six months. The smoked version, pictured here, is smoked over oak in a traditional kiln, giving the rind a brown color. Aside from smoked, the cheese is available in other flavored versions: black pepper and chives, garlic and chives, and garlic and herbs.

SIZE	
D. 8in (20cm)	
H. 4in (10cm)	
WEIGHT	
6½ lb (3kg)	
SHAPE Wheel	
MILK Unpasteurized cow's	
RENNET Vegetarian	
TYPE Modern	

LAMMAS CEREDIGION

Caws Celtica make this Welsh cheese using unpasteurized milk from its flock of sheep. The cheese is matured for at least a month, at which point it has a creamy, moist texture; as it matures, it becomes drier and the flavor more pronounced. It has a golden-brown natural rind and a pale paste with a noticeable taste of sheep. It is also available flavored with spices, including celery seeds, cumin, and black pepper.

SIZE	
D. 3¼–10in (8–25cm)	
H. 2½–3½in (6–9cm)	
WEIGHT	
9oz–10lb (250g–4.5kg)	
SHAPE Round & wheel	
MILK Unpasteurized cow's	
RENNET Vegetarian	
TYPE Modern	

LANARK WHITE LANARKSHIRE

This cheese is made at Walston Braehead in Scotland by Humphrey Errington, using unpasteurized milk from his own ewes. Noted for his blue cheeses, Humphrey drew here on the tradition of unpressed farmhouse cheeses. The sheep's milk curd is drained, molded, unpressed, and matured for three months. As its name suggests, it is indeed a white cheese, with a moist creamy paste and a fresh, citrus tang.

SIZE	
D. 8½in (22cm)	
H. 4in (10cm)	
WEIGHT	
6½lb (3kg)	
SHAPE Wheel	
MILK Unpasteurized sheep's	
RENNET Vegetarian	
TYPE Modern	

LANCASHIRE LANCASHIRE

ONE OF BRITAIN'S "TERRITORIAL" CHEESES, Lancashire developed its own identity in the 18th century, distinguishing itself from neighboring Cheshire. Traditional Lancashire has the softest texture of all England's hard-pressed cow's milk cheeses. Uniquely among English cheeses, it was produced by mixing batches of curds from two or three days' milking. One reason for this is thought to be the small size of Lancashire herds, with farmers unable to gather enough milk in a single day to make such large cheeses.

The 20th century saw the industrialization of Lancashire, like so many other cheeses, and in 1913, the first dairy producing Lancashire opened in Chipping. During World War II, Lancashire was one of the cheeses banned from production; while 202 farms produced Lancashire in 1939, only 22 continued the tradition by 1948, and the number had dwindled to just seven by 1970.

TYPES OF LANCASHIRE

In Lancashire itself, the cheese is widely eaten in two forms: "Creamy" (a young variety, aged for 4–12 weeks) or "Tasty" (aged for 12–24 weeks). The 1970s saw the development of factory-made "Crumbly" or "New" Lancashire, an acidic, firm-textured cheese made from a single day's curd. Sold very young, New Lancashire offered factories a speedier return than the traditional cheese with its longer maturing period, and today this factory-made version dominates production. The Kirkhams at Goosnargh make a traditional farmhouse variety, while Singletons Dairy has obtained a Protected Designation of Origin (PDO) for its Beacon Fell Traditional Lancashire.

KIRKHAM'S LANCASHIRE

SIZE	
D. 12¼in (31cm)	
H. 9in (23cm)	
WEIGHT	
44lb (20kg)	
SHAPE Round	
MILK Unpasteurized cow's	
RENNET Traditional animal	
TYPE Traditional	

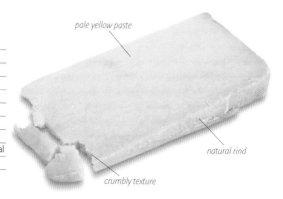

pale yellow paste

natural rind

crumbly texture

KIRKHAM'S LANCASHIRE

The Kirkhams at Goosnargh make this Lancashire with unpasteurized cow's milk and animal rennet. It is produced from the curd of three days' milking, with the clothbound butter-finished cheese matured for six weeks. It has a unique moist yet crumbly texture and a fresh, salty taste with a tang.

LINCOLNSHIRE POACHER
LINCOLNSHIRE

This intriguing mixture between a farmhouse Cheddar and Swiss mountain cheese is made by Simon Jones at Ulceby Grange, Alford. The curd is "Cheddared" and passed through a chip mill. The molded pressed cheese is matured for 15–20 months. Under the natural rind, the smooth yellow paste has a full, nutty, tasty flavor.

SIZE	
D. 12in (30cm)	
H. 9in (23cm)	
WEIGHT	
44lb (20kg)	
SHAPE	Truckle
MILK	Unpasteurized cow's
RENNET	Traditional animal
TYPE	Modern

LITTLE DERBY WARWICKSHIRE

This cheese is made by Fowlers of Earlswood, makers of Derby cheese since 1940. Since the Fowlers moved to Warwickshire in 1918, the cheese became known as "Little Derby," a name applied to Derby cheese made outside of Derbyshire. The cheese is matured for seven months, and washed in red wine to create the distinctive orange exterior. The smooth, moist yellow paste has a mild, buttery flavor.

SIZE	
D. 15in (38cm)	
H. 4in (10cm)	
WEIGHT	
24lb (11kg)	
SHAPE	Round
MILK	Pasteurized cow's
RENNET	Traditional animal
TYPE	Modern

LITTLE HEREFORD HEREFORDSHIRE

This is made today by Monkland Cheese Dairy following a recipe created for small dairies in the county in 1918 by Ellen Yeld. During the making process, "fingers" of curd are pressed together for three days, creating the characteristic open texture. The cheese is matured for four to five months, during which time it develops a pale golden natural rind. The pale yellow paste has a creamy texture and a full, long-lasting flavor.

SIZE	
D. 12in (30cm)	
H. 4in (10cm)	
WEIGHT	
10lb (4.5kg)	
SHAPE	Flat cylinder
MILK	Unpasteurized cow's
RENNET	Vegetarian
TYPE	Modern

LITTLE URN WORCESTERSHIRE

Named after England's 2005 Ashes victory over the Australian cricket team, this sheep cheese is made by Lightwood Cheese. The cut curd is heated, shaped in cloth-lined molds, dipped in hot water, pressed, and matured for 8–12 months. Little Urn has a golden natural rind and a dry-textured, pale golden paste. The flavor is mild with a lingering nutty sweetness and has a hint of sheep to it.

SIZE	
D. 8in (20cm)	
H. 5in (13cm)	
WEIGHT	
8½lb (3.8 kg)	
SHAPE	Cylindrical truckle
MILK	Unpasteurized sheep's
RENNET	Vegetarian
TYPE	Modern

LLANBOIDY DYFED

Llanboidy Cheesemakers have been making this for 25 years using the milk from its Red Poll cows, but more recently sourcing it from a local cooperative. The curd is cut, blocked, piled, milled, and salted before being packed into molds and pressed, helping it to develop a natural rind. The yellow paste has a smooth, firm texture and a mild flavor when young, developing a tang as it ages.

SIZE	
D. 8½in (22cm)	
H. 3¼in (8cm)	
WEIGHT	
9lb (4kg)	
SHAPE Wheel	
MILK Pasteurized cow's	
RENNET Vegetarian	
TYPE Modern	

LLANGLOFFAN PEMBROKESHIRE

Made originally with unpasteurized cow's milk, this Welsh cheese was created by Leon Downey of Llangloffan Farmhouse Cheese. Today, Carmarthenshire Cheese Company makes it using locally sourced milk. The pressed, molded cheese is matured for three to four months. It develops a natural rind over a pale yellow paste. Mild and mellow, it is also available smoked, with garlic and chives, and "red" (with annatto).

SIZE	
D. 8½in (22cm)	
H. 3in (7.5cm)	
WEIGHT	
9lb (4kg)	
SHAPE Round	
MILK Unpasteurized cow's	
RENNET Vegetarian	
TYPE Modern	

LOCH ARTHUR **DUMFRIES**

This is made by the Loch Arthur Community creamery using unpasteurized milk from its cows and local organic herds. It is a clothbound, Cheddar-style cheese, with the curd "Cheddared," milled, pressed, and matured for six months. The matured cheese has a textured rich orange-brown rind, splotched with white mold. The rich golden yellow paste has a smooth texture and full savory flavor with a tangy sharpness.

SIZE	
D. 9½in (24cm)	
H. 11in (28cm)	
WEIGHT	
19½–21lb (8.8–9.5kg)	
SHAPE Cylinder	
MILK Unpasteurized organic cow's	
RENNET Vegetarian	
TYPE Modern	

LOOSEHANGER **WILTSHIRE**

Loosehanger Farmhouse Cheeses at Home Farm, Salisbury, makes this cheese using Ayrshire milk supplied from a single herd, grazed on the Hampshire Downs. During the making, the curd is washed and only lightly pressed before being matured for six to eight weeks. The matured cheese has a dark yellow rind and a moist yellow paste with a scattering of holes. The texture is supple, and the cheese has a mild, mellow flavor.

SIZE	
D. 8¼in (21cm)	
H. 3½in (9cm)	
WEIGHT	
6½lb (3kg)	
SHAPE Round	
MILK Pasteurized cow's	
RENNET Vegetarian	
TYPE Modern	

LORD OF THE HUNDREDS
EAST SUSSEX

This is made by the Traditional Cheese Dairy using unpasteurized sheep's milk. The molded cheese is brined and matured for four to six months, and it develops a textured golden brown natural rind over a smooth, firm pale paste dotted with holes. It has a dry texture and a mild, nutty flavor with a slight aftertaste of sheep.

SIZE	
D. 7–9½in (18–24cm)	
H. 3–4½in (7.5–11cm)	
WEIGHT	
5½–10½lb (2.5–4.8kg)	
SHAPE Square	
MILK Unpasteurized sheep's	
RENNET Vegetarian	
TYPE Modern	

LYBURN GOLD WILTSHIRE

Lyburn Farmhouse Cheesemakers near Salisbury makes this cheese using pasteurized cow's milk from its own herd. During the making process, the curd is washed, then the molded cheese is pressed. Lyburn Gold is matured for around 14 weeks, during which time it develops a golden natural rind. The paste is pale yellow, pocked with a few holes, and has a moist, supple texture with a mellow, sweet flavor.

SIZE	
D. 9in (23cm)	
H. 7in (18cm)	
WEIGHT	
10lb (4.5kg)	
SHAPE Round	
MILK Pasteurized cow's	
RENNET Vegetarian	
TYPE Modern	

MAISIE'S KEBBUCK LANARKSHIRE

Humphrey Errington of Walston Braehead created this cheese for his mother-in-law, Maisie, who is not fond of blue cheese—for which Humphrey is especially known. Inspired by the tradition of Scottish farm cheeses before Cheddar techniques, this is an unpressed cheese, matured for three months, with a natural rind. The pale yellow paste has a moist, crumbly texture and a mild, fresh flavor.

SIZE	
D. 8½in (22cm)	
H. 4in (10cm)	
WEIGHT	
6½lb (3kg)	
SHAPE Wheel	
MILK Unpasteurized cow's	
RENNET Vegetarian	
TYPE Modern	

PROTECTING CHEESE VARIETIES

In France, traditionally produced cheeses have long been protected by a legal system known as the *Appellation d'origine contrôlée* (AOC). This system guarantees that a product of quality was produced in a particular region following established methods. In Britain, by contrast, there has been very little protection for traditionally produced cheeses, with Stilton being one of the few to have been given guidelines on how and where it can be produced. The name Cheddar, for example, can be used by a factory producer of block-made, plastic-wrapped cheese and by a farmhouse cheesemaker making a traditional, cloth-wrapped Cheddar using milk from the farm's own herd.

Increasingly, cheesemakers are seeking protection through European Union (EU) legislation. The Protected Designation of Origin (PDO) covers foodstuffs produced, processed, and prepared in a given geographical area using recognized expertise, while Protected Geographical Indication (PGI) recognizes a geographical link. Cheeses defined by PDOs include Single Gloucester and Swaledale, while Exmoor Blue has PGI status.

MENALLACK FARMHOUSE
CORNWALL

Menallack Farmhouse in Treverna, Penryn, makes this cheese using unpasteurized cow's milk. The curd is molded, pressed for three days, then matured for one to three months, depending on the size of the cheese. It develops a brown natural rind over a firm pale yellow paste, and has a mild, mellow taste; there are also flavored varieties.

SIZE	
D. 4½–12in (11–30cm)	
H. 2½–3½in (6–9cm)	
WEIGHT	
1lb 2oz–15½lb (500g–7kg)	
SHAPE Round	
MILK Unpasteurized cow's	
RENNET Vegetarian	
TYPE Modern	

MILLSTONE SOMERSET

Wootton Organic Dairy makes this cheese using unpasteurized milk from its own sheep. The cheese is unpressed and matured for three to four months, developing a roughly textured, golden brown natural rind splotched with white mold over the firm ivory-colored paste. When young, the flavor is mild; eaten at its peak at around seven to eight months, it has a full salty-sweet flavor and a touch of sharpness.

SIZE	
D. 6–7½in (15–19.5cm)	
H. 3–4in (7.5–10cm)	
WEIGHT	
3lb 3oz–4½lb (1.5–2kg)	
SHAPE Basket	
MILK Unpasteurized organic sheep's	
RENNET Vegetarian	
TYPE Modern	

MONKLAND HEREFORDSHIRE

Made by Monkland Cheese Dairy, this cheese uses a recipe developed by the talented, pioneering cheesemaker James Aldridge. It is an unpressed washed-rind cheese, formed in a flat-bottomed colander which gives it a distinctive shape. Matured for two months, the cheese has an orange rind that is coated with white mold and a moist, pale paste with a long-lasting savory flavor and lemony finish.

SIZE	
D. 6in (15cm)	
H. 3in (7.5cm)	
WEIGHT	
2¼–4½lb (1–2 kg)	
SHAPE Oval	
MILK Unpasteurized cow's	
RENNET Vegetarian	
TYPE Modern	

MOUNT CALLAN CO CLARE

Mount Callan Farmhouse Cheese makes this using unpasteurized milk from the farm's Friesians only during the summer, when the milk is at its richest. Made as a traditional farmhouse Cheddar recipe, it is pressed, clothbound, and matured for 9–18 months, developing a natural rind over a deep yellow paste. The flavor, especially of the longest-matured, is full and powerful with a lingering savoriness.

SIZE	
D. 6in (15cm) & 12in (30cm)	
H. 5in (13cm) & 15in (38cm)	
WEIGHT	
9lb (4kg) & 33lb (15kg)	
SHAPE Truckle	
MILK Unpasteurized cow's	
RENNET Traditional animal	
TYPE Modern	

MR HOLMES'S POMFRIT
YORKSHIRE

Created by cheesemongers Cryer and Stott, this novelty cheese draws on the Yorkshire heritage of licorice-making. Marinated in a mixture of licorice liquor and honey, it is a four-week-old Wensleydale-style cheese. It has a dark brown coat over a moist, crumbly white paste with a mild flavor, contrasting with the sweet licorice taste.

SIZE	
D. 6½in (16cm)	
H. 2in (5cm)	
WEIGHT	
2¼lb (1kg)	
SHAPE	Half-moon
MILK	Pasteurized cow's
RENNET	Vegetarian
TYPE	Modern

MULL OF KINTYRE ARGYLL

The Campbeltown Creamery, housed in a former distillery on the Kintyre peninsula, produces this cheese using pasteurized local cow's milk sourced from within a 10-mile radius. The cheese is made in a large block from a Cheddar recipe for 10–14 months, then cut out from the block and hand-coated with wax. Under the wax coating, the pale yellow paste has a moist texture and a buttery flavor.

SIZE	
D. 3¼in (8cm)	
H. 1½in (4cm)	
WEIGHT	
8oz (225g)	
SHAPE	Round
MILK	Pasteurized cow's
RENNET	Vegetarian
TYPE	Modern

NORFOLK DAPPLE NORFOLK

Ferndale Norfolk Farmhouse Cheese makes this hard-pressed cheese using locally sourced unpasteurized cow's milk. The larger version is made using animal rennet. The curd is molded, pressed, and matured for three to five months, depending on the size. It develops a golden-brown natural rind over a firm pale yellow paste, and has a mild, mellow flavor. It is also available flavored with seeds and peppercorns.

SIZE	
D. 4in (10cm) & 8in (20cm)	
H. 3½in (9cm)	
WEIGHT	
9lb (4kg) & 26½lb (12kg)	
SHAPE Round	
MILK Unpasteurized cow's	
RENNET Traditional animal & vegetarian	
TYPE Modern	

NORSWORTHY DEVON

This cheese is made by Norsworthy Dairy in Crediton using unpasteurized milk from the dairy's own herd of goats. The cheese is based on a Dutch recipe, with the curd washed during the making. Matured for a month, it has a golden-brown rind over a white paste with a mild goaty flavor. When milk supplies permit, the dairy matures some Norsworthy for six to seven months, which lets it develop a fuller flavor.

SIZE	
D. 7in (18cm)	
H. 4½in (11cm)	
WEIGHT	
4½–5½lb (2–2.5kg)	
SHAPE Round	
MILK Unpasteurized goat's	
RENNET Vegetarian	
TYPE Modern	

NORTHUMBERLAND
NORTHUMBERLAND

The Northumberland Cheese Company makes this cheese using locally sourced cow's milk from traceable herds. Made in the Gouda style, the curd is scalded, washed, molded, and brine-bathed, then matured for 12 weeks. It has a smooth, moist texture and mild, creamy flavor. It is also available in flavored versions.

SIZE	
D. 9in (20cm)	
H. 7½in (3cm)	
WEIGHT	
4½–5½lb (2–2.5kg)	
SHAPE Round	
MILK Pasteurized cow's	
RENNET Vegetarian	
TYPE Modern	

OGLESHIELD SOMERSET

Jamie Montgomery makes this shield-shaped cheese using unpasteurized milk from his Jersey cows. The recipe for this cheese was developed with William Oglethorpe, a fact reflected in the cheese's name. During making, the curd is washed and, as the cheese matures, its rind is brine-washed. Matured for four months, it has a sticky orange rind and a smooth yellow paste with a rich, full, fruity flavor.

SIZE	
D. 12½in (32cm)	
H. 3½in (9cm)	
WEIGHT	
12¼lb (5.5kg)	
SHAPE Disc	
MILK Unpasteurized cow's	
RENNET Traditional animal	
TYPE Modern	

OISIN GOAT CO LIMERICK

Rochus and Rose van der Vaard of Oisin Farmhouse Cheese make this cheese during the spring and summer months using milk from their own goats, which graze the mountain pastures. It is a Gouda-style cheese, reflecting Rochus's Dutch roots, with the curd washed, pressed, and matured for 3–18 months. When young, the white paste is supple and mildly nutty; as it ages, it becomes drier with a fuller flavor.

SIZE	
D. 8in (20cm)	
H. 6in (15cm)	
WEIGHT	
9lb (4kg)	
SHAPE Round	
MILK Pasteurized goat's	
RENNET Vegetarian	
TYPE Modern	

OLD WINCHESTER WILTSHIRE

Lyburn Farmhouse Cheesemakers makes this cheese using unpasteurized milk from its cows. As its name suggests, it is a matured version of Lyburn's Winchester cheese, a hard-pressed cheese, carefully matured until it reaches 16–18 months. It has a deep golden rind and a deep yellow paste with a texture that, while flaky and crumbly, is also moist. The flavor is intensely savory with a long-lasting salty-sweet finish.

SIZE	
D. 9in (23cm)	
H. 3in (7.5cm)	
WEIGHT	
9lb (4kg)	
SHAPE Round	
MILK Unpasteurized cow's	
RENNET Vegetarian	
TYPE Modern	

OLD WORCESTER WHITE
WORCESTERSHIRE

Named after the county in which it is made, this hard cheese is produced by Ansteys at Broomhall Farm. During making, the curd is cut into small blocks, which are molded and pressed. Matured for six months, it develops a brown natural rind, blotched with white mold, and a firm pale yellow paste. The flavor is subtle with a milky nuttiness.

SIZE	
D. 8in (20cm)	
H. 6in (15cm)	
WEIGHT	
7½lb (3.5kg)	
SHAPE Round	
MILK Pasteurized cow's	
RENNET Vegetarian	
TYPE Modern	

OLDE GLOSTER   GLOUCESTERSHIRE

This clothbound hard cheese, based on a Double Gloucester recipe, is made by Lightwood Cheese using unpasteurized cow's milk. In order to retain more moisture in the cheese, the curd is scalded at a lower heat and not cut too small. Carrot juice and annatto are added for color and flavor. Matured for seven months, the cheese has a dark orange rind, bright orange paste, and a full, sweet taste with an after-tang.

SIZE	
D. 8in (20cm)	
H. 5in (13cm)	
WEIGHT	
15lb (6.8kg)	
SHAPE Cylindrical truckle	
MILK Unpasteurized cow's	
RENNET Vegetarian	
TYPE Modern	

OLDE SUSSEX **EAST SUSSEX**

The Traditional Cheese Dairy in Wadhurst makes this hard cheese using unpasteurized cow's milk sourced from local farms and dairies. The curd is cut, drained, molded, pressed, and matured for three to four months, during which time it develops a natural rind, coated with white mold. The smooth yellow paste has a moist, open texture, and the flavor is mild with a sweet nuttiness to it.

SIZE	
D. 9½in (24cm)	
H. 3in (7.5cm)	
WEIGHT	
9½lb (4.3kg)	
SHAPE Cylinder	
MILK Unpasteurized cow's	
RENNET Vegetarian	
TYPE Modern	

ORKNEY **ORKNEY ISLANDS**

Hilda Seator at Grimbister Farm on the Isle of Orkney makes this Scottish cheese using unpasteurized milk from the farm's own herd of Friesian cows. The milk from the farm is curdled, then the curd is drained, cut, molded, and pressed for a day, with the cheese sold while it is still very young. The pale paste has a very crumbly, moist texture, while the flavor is fresh and lactic with a faint citrus kick.

SIZE	
D. 5–7in (13–18cm)	
H. 2½–6in (6–15cm)	
WEIGHT	
1¾–7½lb (700g–3.5kg)	
SHAPE Truckle	
MILK Unpasteurized cow's	
RENNET Vegetarian`	
TYPE Modern	

PENDRAGON SOMERSET

One of a handful of British cheeses that uses buffalo's milk, this is made by the Somerset Cheese Company at Ditcheat Hill Farm. The curds are molded, pressed overnight, and matured for between 4–12 months. During this time, Pendragon develops a brown natural rind and a firm yellow paste with a creamy texture, due to the milk's fat content, and a mild, sweet flavor.

SIZE	
D. 7in (18cm) & 10in (25cm)	
H. 2¾in (7cm)	
WEIGHT	
4½lb (2kg) & 7½lb (3.5kg)	
SHAPE Round	
MILK Pasteurized buffalo's	
RENNET Vegetarian	
TYPE Modern	

PENNARD RIDGE SOMERSET

This flaky-textured goat cheese is made by the Somerset Cheese Company at Ditcheat Hill Farm, and named after the local ridge. Made in the Caerphilly style, the cheese is pressed, then brine-washed for a day, and matured for 8–10 weeks. It has a golden-brown natural rind that is dusted with white mold, and an open-textured white paste with a nutty-sweet taste that has a hint of goat.

SIZE	
D. 7in (18cm) & 10in (25cm)	
H. 2¾in (7cm)	
WEIGHT	
4½lb (2kg) & 7½lb (3.5kg)	
SHAPE Wheel	
MILK Pasteurized goat's	
RENNET Vegetarian	
TYPE Modern	

PENNARD RIDGE RED SOMERSET

The Somerset Cheese Company makes this "goat Red Leicester" at Ditcheat Hill Farm using locally sourced milk. To create a more open-textured cheese, Philip Rainbow scalds the curd at a lower heat than is used for Cheddar and works the curd less. Matured for 4–12 months, it has a brown natural rind, while annatto gives the cheese its distinctive deep orange color. The flavor is nutty-sweet with a touch of goat.

SIZE	
D. 7in (18cm) & 10in (25cm)	
H. 2¾in (7cm)	
WEIGHT	
4½lb (2kg) & 7½lb (3.5kg)	
SHAPE Wheel	
MILK Pasteurized goat's	
RENNET Vegetarian	
TYPE Modern	

PENNARD VALE SOMERSET

This hard goat cheese is made by The Somerset Cheese Company at Ditcheat Hill Farm using locally sourced goat's milk. The curd is molded, pressed overnight, and matured for between 4–12 months. During this time, it develops a brown natural rind that is evenly dusted with white mold, while the waxy-textured paste is white and smooth. The flavor is salty-sweet and nutty with a tang of goat to it.

SIZE	
D. 7in (18cm) & 10in (25cm)	
H. 2¾in (7cm)	
WEIGHT	
4½lb (2kg) & 7½lb (3.5kg)	
SHAPE Wheel	
MILK Pasteurized goat's	
RENNET Vegetarian	
TYPE Modern	

QUICKE'S HARD GOAT DEVON

This is made by Quickes Traditional at Home Farm, Newton St. Cyres, using goat's milk sourced from Devon and Dorset. It is made along similar lines to the Cheddar that Quickes also makes, with the curd scalded, "Cheddared," milled, salted, molded, wrapped in cheesecloth, and matured for 6–10 months. The cheese develops a natural rind over a firm white paste with a sweet nuttiness of flavor.

SIZE	
D. 14in (35.5cm)	
H. 12in (30cm)	
WEIGHT	
53lb (24kg)	
SHAPE Truckle	
MILK Pasteurized goat's	
RENNET Vegetarian	
TYPE Modern	

RED LEICESTER LEICESTERSHIRE

Leicestershire Handmade Cheese Company at Sparkenhoe Farm has revived the making of this traditional cheese in the county in which it originated. It is made with unpasteurized milk from the farm's cows, and colored with annatto to give the paste the traditional deep orange color associated with the cheese. Matured for between three to six months, the clothbound cheese has a firm texture and gentle lactic flavor.

SIZE	
D. 14in (35.5cm) & 18in (46cm)	
H. 5in (13cm) & 7in (18cm)	
WEIGHT	
22lb (10kg) & 44lb (20kg)	
SHAPE Wheel	
MILK Unpasteurized cow's	
RENNET Traditional animal	
TYPE Traditional	

REIVER NORTHUMBERLAND

The Northumberland Cheese Company in Blagdon makes this cheese using pasteurized cow's milk. To create the white-mold layer, *Penicillium candidum* is added to the milk at the beginning of the process. The cheese is molded and pressed, and matured for 10–12 weeks, developing a bumpy natural rind coated in bloomy white mold. The moist yellow paste has a mild flavor with a mushroomy note.

SIZE	
D. 8in (20cm)	
H. 3in (7.5cm)	
WEIGHT	
4½–5½lb (2–2.5kg)	
SHAPE Round	
MILK Pasteurized cow's	
RENNET Vegetarian	
TYPE Modern	

RIBBLESDALE ORIGINAL
NORTH YORKSHIRE

A hard goat cheese made for the Ribblesdale Cheese Company, Horton-in-Ribblesdale, this follows a recipe from its founder, the late Iain Hill. The cheese is aged for two to three months and is coated with a pale wax covering. The firm bright white paste has a crumbly texture and a lactic taste with only a hint of goat.

SIZE	
D. 8in (20cm)	
H. 2½in (6cm)	
WEIGHT	
4½lb (2kg)	
SHAPE Wheel	
MILK Pasteurized goat's	
RENNET Vegetarian	
TYPE Modern	

RINGWELL SOMERSET

Wootton Organic Dairy makes this cheese using locally sourced organic milk from a Jersey herd. An unpressed cheese, it is molded in colanders, giving it a distinctive shape, and matured for at least three to four months. The rough natural rind covers a rich golden yellow paste dotted with holes. The texture is firm but moist, and the cheese has a mild but full flavor with a creamy sweetness to the taste.

SIZE	
D. 6–7½in (15–19.5cm)	
H. 3–4in (7.5–10cm)	
WEIGHT	
3lb 3oz–4½lb (1.5–2kg)	
SHAPE Basket	
MILK Unpasteurized organic cow's	
RENNET Vegetarian	
TYPE Modern	

SHEEP'S MILK WENSLEYDALE
YORKSHIRE

The Wensleydale Creamery makes this version of its classic Wensleydale using locally sourced sheep's milk, in a revival of the ancient tradition started by Cistercian monks, who first brought cheese-making to Yorkshire. The gleaming white paste of this Wensleydale is soft and moist, while the flavor is fresh and mild.

SIZE	
D. (2¾in (7cm)	
H. 4in (10cm)	
WEIGHT	
2½ lb (1.1kg)	
SHAPE Cylinder	
MILK Pasteurized sheep's	
RENNET Vegetarian	
TYPE Traditional	

SHIPCORD SUFFOLK

This hard cow's milk cheese is made by Rodwell Farm Dairy at its farm in Baylham. The unpasteurized cow's milk is curdled, the curd is very finely chopped, and the whey is thoroughly drained off. The pressed, molded cheese is matured for six months and develops a pale brown natural rind over a firm yellow paste with a smooth texture. The flavor is mild, but with a butterscotch sweetness to it.

SIZE	
D. 10in (25cm)	
H. 4in (10cm)	
WEIGHT	
9½–10½lb (4.3–4.8kg)	
SHAPE Round	
MILK Unpasteurized cow's	
RENNET Vegetarian	
TYPE Modern	

TOOLS OF THE TRADE

As in any specialist area of production, cheesemakers use specific tools. Several of these are traditional ones that have changed little in function or design for centuries.

• **Curd knives:** these are used to cut the set curd, releasing the whey. The term is applied to long-bladed fine knives, but also to wire-strung cutters, sometimes called "cheese harps," which can be passed through the vat to cube the curd.

• **Cheese press:** To make a hard-pressed cheese, the curd is placed in a mold and pressed in a press, with the cheesemaker varying the pressure as required.

• **Cheese iron:** this is used to check the progress of a large hard cheese without cutting it. The sample is pulled out, then pushed back in to plug the hole once the cheese has been assessed.

CHEESE IRON
The iron is used to pull out a plug of cheese so that it can be checked.

SINGLE GLOUCESTER
GLOUCESTERSHIRE

Charles Martell revived the making of Single Gloucester, which now has a Protected Designation of Origin (PDO), meaning it can be made only in Gloucestershire on farms with a pedigree herd of Old Gloucesters. Matured for two to three months, it has a pale paste under a moldy natural rind with a soft, creamy texture and a mild lactic flavor.

SIZE	
D. 8½in (22cm)	
H. 2¾in (7cm)	
WEIGHT	
5lb (2.25kg)	
SHAPE Wheel	
MILK Pasteurized cow's	
RENNET Vegetarian	
TYPE Traditional	

SNODSBURY GOAT
WORCESTERSHIRE

Made by Ansteys using unpasteurized goat's milk, the curd is pressed for 48 hours and the clothbound cheese is matured for four months. It has a very pale brown natural rind that is blotched with white mold, and a firm-textured white to ivory-colored paste. The flavor is goaty, but not overpowering, and it has a rich, full nuttiness.

SIZE	
D. 8in (20cm)	
H. 4in (10cm)	
WEIGHT	
4lb (1.8 kg)	
SHAPE Wheel	
MILK Unpasteurized goat's	
RENNET Vegetarian	
TYPE Modern	

SPENWOOD **BERKSHIRE**

Village Maid makes this unpasteurized sheep's milk cheese named after Spencers Wood Village. The drained, molded cheese is matured for six months, in which time it develops a brown natural rind over a gleaming paste. The texture is slightly flaky, while the flavor is nutty with a lingering sweetness. As it matures, the texture of Spenwood becomes harder and drier, and the flavor becomes spicier and fuller.

SIZE

D. 8in (20cm)

H. 3in (7.5cm)

WEIGHT

4½lb (2kg)

SHAPE Round

MILK Unpasteurized sheep's

RENNET Vegetarian

TYPE Modern

ST EGWIN **WORCESTERSHIRE**

This cheese is made by Gorsehill Abbey Cheese using organic milk from its own herd of Friesian and Montbeliarde cows at Gorsehill Abbey Farm. Named after the founder of the local Evesham Abbey, St. Egwin is matured for one to eight months, developing a white-dusted golden rind over a deep yellow paste pocked with holes. The texture is moist and pliable, and it has a mild but lingering nutty sweetness.

SIZE

D. 8in (20cm)

H. 4½in (11cm)

WEIGHT

5lb (2.25kg)

SHAPE Low cylinder

MILK Pasteurized cow's

RENNET Animal

TYPE Modern

ST GALL CO CORK

This Irish cheese is made by the Fermoy Cheese Company using milk from its own Friesians. The curd is heated in copper-lined vats, cut very finely, pressed, brine-bathed, and matured on timber boards, smeared with a brine solution. Matured for five to six months, it has a golden-orange rind, a spicy aroma, and a smooth deep yellow paste, dotted with tiny bubbles. The flavor is rich, mellow, and lingering.

SIZE	
D. 12in (30cm)	
H. 4in (10cm)	
WEIGHT	
10½lb (4.8kg)	
SHAPE Wheel	
MILK Unpasteurized cow's	
RENNET Traditional animal	
TYPE Modern	

ST KENELM WORCESTERSHIRE

Gorsehill Abbey Cheese at Gorsehill Abbey Farm makes this cheese, named after an ancient king of Mercia, using organic milk from its own cows. The cheese is matured for two to six months, developing a natural rind over the rich yellow paste. The texture is firm but moist with a creaminess to it and a mild flavor, although as the cheese matures, this takes on more of a tang.

SIZE	
D. 8in (20cm)	
H. 4½in (11cm)	
WEIGHT	
5lb (2.25kg)	
SHAPE Low cylinder	
MILK Pasteurized cow's	
RENNET Traditional animal	
TYPE Modern	

SUSSEX SCRUMPY EAST SUSSEX

The Traditional Cheese Dairy in Wadhurst makes this cheese using unpasteurized milk sourced from local farms and dairies. Made in the Cheddar style, a mixture of cider, herbs, and garlic is added to the paste, and the cheese is matured for three months. The creamy-textured pale yellow paste is flecked with green, and the cheese has a savory, garlicky flavor with the sweetness of the cider also noticeable.

SIZE	
D. 9½in (24cm)	
H. 3in (7.5cm)	
WEIGHT	
4½lb (2kg)	
SHAPE Half-moon	
MILK Pasteurized cow's	
RENNET Vegetarian	
TYPE Modern	

SUSSEX YEOMAN EAST SUSSEX

Nut Knowle Farm in Horam makes this hard-pressed cheese using pasteurized milk from its herd of Toggenburg and British Saanen goats. The curd is finely cut, scalded, molded, pressed, and brined, then matured for two months. During maturation, it develops a textured, golden-brown natural rind over a white paste, which has a slightly moist and crumbly texture. The flavor is mild and nutty-sweet.

SIZE	
D. 7in (18cm)	
H. 3½in (9cm)	
WEIGHT	
4½lb (2kg)	
SHAPE Wheel	
MILK Pasteurized goat's	
RENNET Vegetarian	
TYPE Modern	

SWALEDALE GOAT YORKSHIRE

Swaledale cheese has traditionally been made in the Yorkshire Dales for centuries, with this hard goat cheese being made by the Swaledale Cheese Company. The goat's milk curd is milled, molded, pressed, bathed in brine overnight, and matured for six weeks, during which time it is brushed and turned. It has a grayish-brown natural rind and a firm white paste, which has a salty-sweet, goaty flavor.

SIZE	
D. 6½in (16cm)	
H. 3¼in (8cm)	
WEIGHT	
5½lb (2.5kg)	
SHAPE Round	
MILK Pasteurized goat's	
RENNET Vegetarian	
TYPE Modern	

SWEET CHARLOTTE DEVON

This hard cheese is made for Country Cheeses by Rachel Stephens of Curworthy Cheeses using milk from her own herd of Friesians and a starter culture used for Jarlsberg and Emmental cheeses. Matured for six to eight months, the cheese develops a rich golden rind over a yellow paste dotted with tiny holes. The texture is smooth and slippery, while the flavor is rich and full with a long-lasting finish.

SIZE	
D. 7in (18cm)	
H. 3½in (9cm)	
WEIGHT	
6½lb (3kg)	
SHAPE Round	
MILK Pasteurized cow's	
RENNET Vegetarian	
TYPE Modern	

TEIFI CEREDIGION

John Savage of Teifi Farmhouse Cheese makes this cheese using unpasteurized cow's milk from a single herd. The cheese is matured for 12 weeks–2 years, depending on size. It has a golden rind and a smooth yellow paste. When young, Teifi is sweet and buttery; when aged, it becomes drier and flakier with a stronger taste. It is available in flavored versions, including cumin, a nod to John's Dutch ancestry.

SIZE	
D. 4–16in (10–40cm)	
H. 2½–6in (6–15cm)	
WEIGHT	
1lb 2oz–26½lb (500g–12kg)	
SHAPE Wheel	
MILK Unpasteurized cow's	
RENNET Vegetarian	
TYPE Modern	

TICKLEMORE DEVON

Ticklemore cheese was originally created and made by cheesemaker Robin Congdon of Ticklemore Cheeses. Nowadays, however, the cheese is made on the Sharpham Estate by Debbie Mumford, who used to work with Robin. The cheese has a textured rind from the baskets in which it is formed and a fine white paste, dotted with holes. The paste is moist and crumbly, and has a subtle, fresh flavor.

SIZE	
D. 7in (18cm)	
H. 3¼in (8cm)	
WEIGHT	
3lb 3oz (1.5kg)	
SHAPE Basket	
MILK Pasteurized goat's	
RENNET Vegetarian	
TYPE Modern	

TREHILL DEVON

This flavored cheese is made for Country Cheeses by Rachel Stephens using milk from her herd of Friesian cows. Garlic and chives are added to the curd, which is then molded, pressed, and brined. It is matured for three to four months. A dark green wax coating covers a moist yellow paste flecked with dark green flakes, and the texture is creamy with the flavor of garlic and chives dominating the cheese.

SIZE	
D. 3 ½in (9cm) & 7½in (19.5cm)	
H. 2in (5cm) & 3in (7.5cm)	
WEIGHT	
14oz (400g) & 5lb (2.2kg)	
SHAPE Round	
MILK Pasteurized cow's	
RENNET Vegetarian	
TYPE Modern	

TRELAWNY CORNWALL

Whalesborough Farm Foods near Bude makes this hard cheese from pasteurized cow's milk. The molded curd is pressed for 24 hours, and the cheese is matured for six to eight weeks, during which time it develops a grayish-brown natural rind that is splotched with pink mold from the dairy in which it is made. The pale yellow paste has a firm texture and a balanced yet lingering flavor.

SIZE	
D. 8in (20cm)	
H. 4in (10cm)	
WEIGHT	
3lb 3oz (1.5kg)	
SHAPE Wheel	
MILK Pasteurized cow's	
RENNET Vegetarian	
TYPE Modern	

CLOTHBOUND CHEESES

A characteristic of traditional British cheese-making is the practice of wrapping cheese in muslin, so that it is protected but allowed to breathe as it matures.

TREMAINS SUSSEX

High Weald Dairy in Horsted Keynes make this organic Cheddar cheese, named after the farm where the cheese is made. To make the cheese, the curd is cut, milled, molded, and pressed, then set aside to mature for at least three months. The matured cheese has a golden natural rind and a pale yellow paste with a smooth, creamy texture and a full flavor with a tang to it.

SIZE	
D. 9.5in (24cm)	
H. 2¾–3¼in (7–8cm)	
WEIGHT	
6½lb (3kg)	
SHAPE Round	
MILK Pasteurized organic cow's	
RENNET Vegetarian	
TYPE Modern	

VILLAGE GREEN CORNWALL

Cornish Country Larder makes this hard goat cheese at its creamery near Padstow in Cornwall, using goat's milk sourced from a number of farms that supply to the creamery. The cheese is matured for six months and is coated in a bright green wax covering, contrasting with the bright white interior. The paste is crumbly and moist, and the cheese has a mild flavor with only a hint of goat to it.

SIZE	
D. 3½in (9cm)	
H. 2¾in (7cm)	
WEIGHT	
2¾lb (1.25kg)	
SHAPE Block	
MILK Pasteurized goat's	
RENNET Vegetarian	
TYPE Modern	

WARWICKSHIRE TRUCKLE
WEST MIDLANDS

Fowlers of Earlswood has been making this cheese for more than 70 years. The scalded curd is milled, molded, and pressed before being clothbound and waxed. Matured for seven months, it has a firm, moist yellow paste with a mild flavor. It is available in flavored versions layered with garlic and parsley, chile, or black pepper.

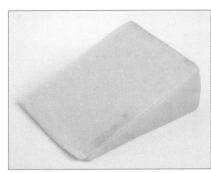

SIZE	
D. 8in (20cm)	
H. 8in (20cm)	
WEIGHT	
13lb (6kg)	
SHAPE Truckle	
MILK Pasteurized cow's	
RENNET Vegetarian	
TYPE Traditional	

WEDMORE SOMERSET

Duckett's, best known for its Caerphilly, makes this cheese at Westcombe Dairy, near Shepton Mallet. While the curd is being placed in the molds, a layer of chopped chives is added. Matured for only two weeks, the cheese does not develop a rind. It is a pale cream-colored cheese, marked with a band of green, with a crumbly, moist texture. The salty mildness of the cheese contrasts with the onion flavor of chives.

SIZE	
D. 6¾in (17cm)	
H. 3in (7.5cm)	
WEIGHT	
4½lb (2kg)	
SHAPE Wheel	
MILK Pasteurized cow's	
RENNET Vegetarian	
TYPE Modern	

WENSLEYDALE YORKSHIRE

A HISTORIC YORKSHIRE CHEESE, Wensleydale originated with French Cistercian monks from the Roquefort region who came to England with William the Conqueror. The monks settled in the Yorkshire Dales, building first a monastery at Fors in 1150AD, then an abbey at Jervaulx in Lower Wensleydale. The monks made cheese from the local ewes' milk and used mold from local stone to create a blue version. Their knowledge spread to the surrounding populace, and even after the monasteries were dissolved under Henry VIII, the monks' traditional cheese continued to thrive. The use of the name "Wensleydale" for the cheese has been traced back to 1840, when grocers could buy a soft-textured, moist blue-veined cheese at annual cheese fairs.

PRODUCING WENSLEYDALE

By the mid-17th century, cow's milk had replaced sheep's in most British cheeses, and Wensleydale was no exception. In the late 19th century, Edward Chapman, a provision merchant and major buyer of farmhouse Wensleydale, set up a Wensleydale Cheese Factory, making a white cheese with a firmer texture than the traditional farmhouse variety. During World War II, the Ministry of Food ordered that only Chapman's harder, longer-lasting version could be produced, and farmhouse Wensleydale largely disappeared.

Today, Wensleydale Dairy Products at Hawes Creamery is the only company that continues to make the cheese in Wensleydale itself. Classic Wensleydale has a pale white paste, a distinctive flaky, moist texture, and a delicate sweetness of flavor. In Yorkshire, Wensleydale is often eaten with sweet foods such as fruit cake.

HAWES'S WENSLEYDALE

SIZE	
D. 7in (18cm)	
H. 7in (18cm)	
WEIGHT	
11lb (5kg)	
SHAPE	Truckle
MILK	Pasteurized cow's
RENNET	Traditional animal or vegetarian
TYPE	Traditional

flaky and moist

cream-colored paste

HAWES'S WENSLEYDALE

Hawes Creamery in Wensleydale makes this cheese using locally sourced cow's milk. To create the characteristic flaky, moist texture, the cheese is only lightly pressed. Matured for four to six months, it has a cream-colored paste and a delicate taste. It is also available in flavored versions.

WHITE STILTON NOTTINGHAMSHIRE

White Stilton, although made by Stilton makers, is an unveined cheese, with no *Penicillium roqueforti* added to the milk or piercing of the cheese during maturing. An unpressed cheese, this white Stilton is made by Cropwell Bishop Creamery, sold while very young. The pale paste is crumbly and moist, with a fresh, mild flavor. It is available in a number of flavored versions, including cranberry and blueberry.

SIZE	
D. 8in (20cm)	
H. 10in (25cm)	
WEIGHT	
17½lb (8kg)	
SHAPE Cylinder	
MILK Pasteurized cow's	
RENNET Vegetarian	
TYPE Modern	

WILD GARLIC YARG CORNWALL

Lynher Dairy at Pengreep Farm makes this flavored cheese using cow's milk from the dairy's own herd and neighboring farms. The molded cheeses are brine-washed overnight, dried, then covered with wild garlic leaves. As the cheese matures, a sprinkling of white mold grows on the green leaf wrapping. Once ready to eat, it has a moist, creamy-textured white paste with a mild garlic flavor.

SIZE	
D. 7¼in (19cm)	
H. 2¾in (7cm)	
WEIGHT	
3¾lb (1.7kg)	
SHAPE Wheel	
MILK Pasteurized cow's	
RENNET Vegetarian	
TYPE Modern	

WOOLSERY ENGLISH GOAT
DORSET

Woolsery Cheese makes this cheese using Dorset-sourced pasteurized goat's milk. The curd is drained, molded, and pressed in Victorian cheese presses, then matured for 8–12 weeks. It develops a brown natural rind over a smooth white paste. The texture is firm, yet moist, and it has a salty-nutty taste with only a hint of goat.

SIZE
D. 2½in (6cm)
H. 2½in (6cm)
WEIGHT
5lb (2.2kg)
SHAPE Round
MILK Pasteurized goat's
RENNET Vegetarian
TYPE Modern

THE BRITISH CHEESE AWARDS

In 1994, Juliet Harbutt, a noted cheese expert, established the British Cheese Awards with the aims of raising the standards of British cheese and creating a symbol of excellence. In its inaugural year, 97 cheesemakers entered fewer than 300 cheeses. By 2007, 175 cheesemakers submitted almost 900 cheeses, proving how much the event had grown. Cheeses are submitted within a large variety of categories, including by type (such as blue, fresh, soft), "Best Organic," and other categories, such as "Best Scottish." The cheeses are judged in the summer by a panel from around the world, and the winners are announced at the autumn Awards Dinner. There are winners in each category and one overall Supreme Champion. Winning an award here is a source of great pride for cheesemakers.

Harbutt runs other events to promote British cheeses: The Great British Cheese Festival is designed to inform the public about the wide variety of British cheeses, and British Cheese Week promotes British cheese in shops and restaurants.

WORCESTERSHIRE SAUCE

WORCESTERSHIRE

Made by Ansteys, this cheese is characterized by the addition of a classic British condiment, Worcestershire sauce, made by nearby Lea & Perrins. Matured for only three months, it has a golden natural rind with white mold, and a pale yellow paste with distinctive purple-brown marbling. The flavor is subtly spicy with a hint of pickles.

SIZE	
D. 8in (20cm)	
H. 6in (15cm)	
WEIGHT	
7½lb (3.5kg)	
SHAPE Round	
MILK Pasteurized cow's	
RENNET Vegetarian	
TYPE Modern	

WYFE OF BATH SOMERSET

Named after Chaucer's pilgrim, this is made by Bath Soft Cheese at Park Farm, Kelston, using milk from the farm's own cows. The cheese is made from unpressed washed curd, then molded in baskets and drained under its own weight. Matured for 10 weeks, it develops a golden natural rind, flecked with white mold. The pale yellow paste has a little bounce to it, and the flavor is mild yet full.

SIZE	
D. 10in (25cm)	
H. 15in (38cm)	
WEIGHT	
6½lb (3kg)	
SHAPE Basket	
MILK Pasteurized cow's	
RENNET Vegetarian	
TYPE Modern	

Y-FENNI GWENT

This flavored cheese is produced by Abergavenny Fine Foods and is named after the Welsh name for Abergavenny, the town in which it is made. The cheese is made by blending mature Cheddar cheese with whole-grain mustard and Welsh ale. The mixture is then molded and coated in wax. The yellow paste, speckled with mustard seeds, has a moist texture and a savory, mildly piquant flavor.

SIZE	
D. 7in (18cm)	
H. 2in (5cm)	
WEIGHT	
3lb 3oz (1.5kg)	
SHAPE	Wheel
MILK	Pasteurized cow's
RENNET	Vegetarian
TYPE	Modern

THE PASTEURIZATION DEBATE

Today, the majority of cheese is made from pasteurized milk, which has been heat-treated—usually to a temperature of 161°F (71.7°C) for 15 seconds—to kill micro-organisms that cause disease and decay. The technique was invented by Louis Pasteur in 1862, and for hundreds of years prior to that, all cheese was made with untreated milk. Pasteurization has gone hand in hand with the industrialization of cheese-making, enabling dairies to transport milk from farms to factories without it souring.

However, many cheesemakers and cheesemongers passionately believe that cheese should be made from raw milk. Pasteurization, they point out, kills not just pathogenic (disease-causing) bacteria, but also harmless micro-organisms that enhance the flavor of cheese. Heat-treated milk tends to be uniform and lacks the depth of flavor found in "raw" milk; it consequently produces less interesting cheese with no sense of place. Health concerns, they argue, are exaggerated: many cheese-related food scares have involved cheese made from pasteurized rather than raw milk, and poor hygiene in the dairy or during maturing poses a much greater threat than natural milk bacteria.

BLUE CHEESES

Easily identified by the veins of blue-green mold that run through them, blue cheeses have a fairly soft texture and a distinctive tang, resulting from the development of mold within the cheese. Stilton is Britain's best-known blue cheese, tracing its history back to the 18th century, but several other notable blues are well worth sampling.

BADENTOY BLUE ABERDEENSHIRE

Devenick Dairy near Aberdeen makes this cheese using pasteurized milk from its herd of dairy cows. *Penicillium roqueforti* is added to the milk at the beginning of the cheese-making process to ensure the development of the veining, and the molded cheese is pierced. Matured for four months, it develops a natural rind over a firm, moist yellow paste with scattered veining. The flavor is only mildly blue.

SIZE	
D. 5¾in (14.5cm)	
H. 3¼in (8cm)	
WEIGHT	
3lb (1.3kg)	
SHAPE	Round
MILK	Pasteurized cow's
RENNET	Vegetarian
TYPE	Modern

BARKHAM BLUE BERKSHIRE

Two Hoots Cheese in Barkham makes this blue cheese using pasteurized Channel Islands' milk, which has a high butterfat content. *Penicillium roqueforti* is added to the milk, with the unpressed, molded cheese pierced at a week old to encourage veining. Matured for five to six weeks, it has a pale yellow paste and blue-green veining. It has a buttery texture and sweet flavor, with a savory note from the veining.

SIZE	
D. 7in (18cm)	
H. 3in (7.5cm)	
WEIGHT	
3lb (1.3kg)	
SHAPE	Round
MILK	Pasteurized cow's
RENNET	Vegetarian
TYPE	Modern

BEENLEIGH BLUE DEVON

Ticklemore Cheeses near Sharpham Barton, pioneer makers of blue sheep's milk cheeses, makes Beenleigh Blue. This unpressed cheese is foil-wrapped once the blue has developed sufficiently, and matured until it is at least five months old. The resulting cheese has a pale paste streaked with blue-green veining. With a crumbly, moist texture and sweet, complex flavor, it has a savoriness from the veining.

SIZE	
D. 8in (20cm)	
H. 4–5in (10–13cm)	
WEIGHT	
6½–7½lb (3–3½kg)	
SHAPE Round	
MILK Pasteurized sheep's	
RENNET Vegetarian	
TYPE Modern	

BELLINGHAM BLUE CO LOUTH

Peter Thomas of Glyde Farm Produce, Castlebellingham, makes this Irish blue cheese using unpasteurized cow's milk from his brother-in-law's herd of Friesians. The unpressed cheese is hand-pierced at two weeks, then ripened for four months. Once matured, it has a pale golden natural rind and a moist cream-colored paste dotted with blue-green mold, and a rich, full, nutty lingering flavor.

SIZE	
D. 8in (20cm)	
H. 3–4½in (7.5–11cm)	
WEIGHT	
6½–9lb (3–4kg)	
SHAPE Round	
MILK Unpasteurized cow's	
RENNET Vegetarian	
TYPE Modern	

BIRDWOOD BLUE HEAVEN
GLOUCESTERSHIRE

Made by Birdwood Farmhouse Cheesemakers, this cheese uses unpasteurized milk from a herd of Shorthorns. *Penicillium roqueforti* is added, and it is matured for at least four weeks, developing a natural crust over a pale yellow paste, blotched with mold. The texture is creamy and yielding, while the flavor has a marked piquancy.

SIZE	
D. 2in (5cm) & 8in (20cm)	
H. 2in (5cm) & 6in (15cm)	
WEIGHT	
14oz (400g) & 3lb 3oz (1.5kg)	
SHAPE Round	
MILK Unpasteurized cow's	
RENNET Vegetarian	
TYPE Modern	

BLACKSTICKS BLUE LANCASHIRE

Blacksticks Blue is made by Butlers Farmhouse Cheese, near Preston, using milk from the farm's herd. To give the cheese its striking bright orange color, annatto is added to the milk, while *Penicillium roqueforti* is used to create the blue-green molding. Once molded, the cheese is pierced to encourage the veining, and it is matured for two months. The soft orange paste has a creamy texture and a buttery tang.

SIZE	
D. 8¼in (21cm)	
H. 2½in (6cm)	
WEIGHT	
5½lb (2.5kg)	
SHAPE Cylinder	
MILK Pasteurized cow's	
RENNET Vegetarian	
TYPE Modern	

BLISSFUL BUFFALO SOMERSET

One of the few British buffalo's milk blue cheeses, this is made by the Exmoor Blue Cheese Company at Willett Farm, Lydeard St. Lawrence. The cheese is matured for four to six weeks, during which time it develops a golden-brown natural rind over an ivory-colored paste that is lightly veined with green-blue mold. The texture is dense and moist, with the milky sweetness of the milk contrasting with the tang of the mold.

SIZE	
D. 5in (13cm)	
H. 3½in (9cm)	
WEIGHT	
2¼lb (1kg)	
SHAPE Cylinder	
MILK Unpasteurized buffalo's	
RENNET Vegetarian	
TYPE Modern	

BLUE CHESHIRE CHESHIRE

H.S. Bourne, whose family has been making Cheshire cheese for generations, makes this traditional cheese using milk from his own cows. It is pressed, pierced, and matured for six to seven months in an old cellar, where the mold in the atmosphere penetrates the cheese. The mature cheese has a natural rind and a flaky, moist paste splotched with blue. The flavor is mild with a gentle spiciness from the blue veining.

SIZE	
D. 9in (23cm)	
H. 9in (23cm)	
WEIGHT	
17½lb (8kg)	
SHAPE Round	
MILK Pasteurized cow's	
RENNET Vegetarian	
TYPE Traditional	

BLUE HILLS SOMERSET

This blue cheese is made for Country Cheeses by cheesemaker Ian Arnett of Exmoor Blue Cheese. Unusually, it is made with a mixture of both cow's and goat's milks. Matured for two months, the cheese develops a distinctive dark brownish-gray rind, coating a pale paste with only a touch of barely visible veining. It has a firm but moist texture and a full flavor with a tangy finish due to the goat's milk.

SIZE	
D. 5in (13cm)	
H. 4in (10cm)	
WEIGHT	
2¼lb (1kg)	
SHAPE Round	
MILK Unpasteurized cow's & goat's	
RENNET Vegetarian	
TYPE Modern	

BLUE WENSLEYDALE YORKSHIRE

The Wensleydale Creamery makes this cheese from locally sourced cow's milk, reviving a tradition of making a blue Wensleydale. To create the blueing, *Penicillium roqueforti* is added, and the molded curd is lightly pressed, with the cheese pierced later on to encourage the veining. Matured for six months, it develops a natural rind over a firm pale paste mottled with veining. The flavor is mellow and savory.

SIZE	
D. 6¾in (17.5cm)	
H. 7½in (19.5cm)	
WEIGHT	
11 lb (5kg)	
SHAPE Round	
MILK Pasteurized cow's	
RENNET Vegetarian	
TYPE Traditional	

BLUE WHINNOW CUMBRIA

Thornby Dairy at Crofton Hall makes this blue cheese using unpasteurized milk from a single herd of Shorthorn cows. *Penicillium roqueforti* is added to the milk to create the veining, and the molded curd is unpressed and pierced to encourage the mold to grow. The cheese is matured for five weeks and best eaten at six weeks. The texture is firm but buttery, and it has a nutty savoriness with a sharp after-tang.

SIZE	
D. 5½in (14cm)	
H. 2¾in (7cm)	
WEIGHT	
2¼lb (1kg)	
SHAPE Flat truckle	
MILK Unpasteurized cow's	
RENNET Vegetarian	
TYPE Modern	

BRENDON BLUE SOMERSET

This blue goat cheese is made by the Exmoor Blue Cheese Company at Willett Farm, Lydeard St. Lawrence, using goat's milk from local herds. *Penicillium roqueforti* is added to the milk to create the blue veining. Matured for four to six weeks, Brendon Blue has a natural rind over a white paste with a dryish, crumbly texture. The flavor combines a goaty freshness with a noticeable tang from the blue.

SIZE	
D. 4½in (11cm)	
H. 4½in (11cm)	
WEIGHT	
2¼lb (1kg)	
SHAPE Cylinder	
MILK Unpasteurized goat's	
RENNET Vegetarian	
TYPE Modern	

BUFFALO BLUE YORKSHIRE

One of a handful of British blue buffalo's milk cheeses, this is made by Shepherds Purse Cheeses, which sources its milk from a local farmer. Matured for 10 weeks, the cheese develops a brown rind, while the ivory paste is scattered with greenish-blue veining. The texture is soft and creamy, and the flavor of the paste is mild with a salty-nuttiness imparted from the veining.

SIZE	
D. 8in (20cm)	
H. 8in (20cm)	
WEIGHT	
6½lb (3kg)	
SHAPE Round	
MILK Pasteurized buffalo's	
RENNET Vegetarian	
TYPE Modern	

CASHEL BLUE CO TIPPERARY

Named after the Rock of Cashel, this cheese was Ireland's first farmhouse blue cheese, created by the Grubbs in 1984. Today, the cheese is still made at their farm near Cashel using milk from their own cows as well as locally sourced milk. After maturing, the firm, moist cream-colored paste is mottled with blue veining. Eaten at around three months, it has a melting, creamy texture and a mellow flavor.

SIZE	
D. 5in (13cm)	
H. 3½in (9cm)	
WEIGHT	
3lb 3oz (1.5kg)	
SHAPE Round	
MILK Pasteurized cow's	
RENNET Vegetarian	
TYPE Modern	

CORNISH BLUE CORNWALL

The Cornish Cheese Company makes this West Country cheese at its farm near Liskeard. *Penicillium roqueforti* is added at the start of the process, and the molded, unpressed cheese is pierced to create the veining. Depending on the size of the cheese, it is matured for between 6–12 weeks. The resulting cheese has a creamy-textured pale yellow paste, blotched with blue veining, and a mild, sweet flavor.

SIZE	
D. 4–11in (10–28cm)	
H. 4–7in (10–18cm)	
WEIGHT	
1lb 2oz–11lb (500g–5kg)	
SHAPE Round	
MILK Pasteurized cow's	
RENNET Vegetarian	
TYPE Modern	

CROZIER BLUE CO TIPPERARY

Available only seasonally, this cheese has been commercially produced since 1999 by the Grubb family in Beechmount near Fethard using locally sourced sheep's milk. A slow-maturing cheese, it has an ivory-colored paste, crumbly when young, which becomes creamier as the cheese ages. The nutty sweetness of the sheep's milk contrasts with the spicy tang of the blue veining.

SIZE	
D. 5in (13cm)	
H. 3½in (9cm)	
WEIGHT	
3lb 3oz (1.5kg)	
SHAPE Round	
MILK Pasteurized sheep's	
RENNET Vegetarian	
TYPE Modern	

DEVON BLUE DEVON

The Ticklemore Cheese Company makes a trio of blue cheeses using milk from different dairy animals, with this one made from locally sourced cow's milk. An unpressed cheese, it is matured until four months old. The resulting cheese has a crumbly, moist pale yellow paste, mottled with blue veining created by the addition of *Penicillium roqueforti*. The flavor is creamy with a rich savoriness.

SIZE	
D. 8in (20cm)	
H. 4–5in (10–13cm)	
WEIGHT	
6½–7½lb (3–3½kg)	
SHAPE Round	
MILK Pasteurized cow's	
RENNET Vegetarian	
TYPE Modern	

DORSET BLUE VINNEY DORSET

Mike Davies of Woodbridge Farm revived the making of this regional cheese (originally made using skim milk) in 1984. Today, his family continues to make it using hand-skimmed unpasteurized milk from the farm's cows, with additional skim milk powder. Matured for three to five months, it has a crumbly pale yellow paste, splotched with blue-green veins, and a mild, long-lasting savoriness.

SIZE	
D. 10in (25cm)	
H. 12in (30cm)	
WEIGHT	
13lb (6kg)	
SHAPE Truckle	
MILK Unpasteurized cow's	
RENNET Vegetarian	
TYPE Traditional	

BACTERIA AND MOLD

Bacteria and mold are generally viewed as something to be avoided, which is why some people may not be comfortable with the idea that cheesemakers actively encourage the growth of certain molds. Cheese is a fermented food and, in this carefully managed process of decay, bacteria and molds play a vital role in creating flavor and texture.

To make blue cheeses, *Penicillium roqueforti* is added to the milk and encouraged to grow. The bloomy white mold rind on some cheeses is created through adding *Penicillium candidum*. A more unusual mold is *Geotrichum candidum*, which affects the cheese's flavor and texture. When making washed-rind cheeses, a solution containing *Brevibacterium linens* creates the characteristic pungent odor.

VEINING
The veining in blue cheese differs, but is always striking.

DUNSYRE BLUE LANARKSHIRE

Humphrey Errington of Walston Braehead Farm makes this blue cheese using unpasteurized Ayrshire milk to which *Penicillium roqueforti* is added. The curd is cut, drained of whey, packed into molds, rubbed with salt, pierced to let the veining develop, and matured for six weeks. The matured cheese has a creamy-textured pale yellow paste, blotched with blue-green molding, which adds a powerful spiciness.

SIZE
D. 6½in (16cm)
H. 4¾in (12cm)
WEIGHT
6½lb (3kg)
SHAPE Wheel
MILK Unpasteurized cow's
RENNET Vegetarian
TYPE Modern

EXMOOR BLUE SOMERSET

Made by Exmoor Blue Cheese Company at Willett Farm, this cheese uses locally sourced unpasteurized milk from Jersey cows—a fact assured by its Protected Geographical Indication (PGI) status, which defines how the cheese is made. Matured for four to six weeks, it develops a natural rind over a soft, blue-veined primrose yellow paste. The sharp, tangy veining contrasts with the buttery creaminess of the paste.

SIZE	
D. 4¾in (12cm) & 7in (18cm)	
H. 2½in (6cm)	
WEIGHT	
1lb 2oz (500g) & 2¾lb (1.25kg)	
SHAPE Round	
MILK Unpasteurized cow's	
RENNET Vegetarian	
TYPE Modern	

FOWLERS FOREST BLUE
DERBYSHIRE

This cheese is made by Fowlers of Earlswood from pasteurized cow's milk. Matured in a humid environment for five months, it has a very thin, brown natural rind over a firm pale yellow paste, which is only lightly marked with green veining. The paste has a mild, salty flavor with a mild tang from the veining.

SIZE	
D. 8in (20cm)	
H. 6in (15cm)	
WEIGHT	
11lb (5kg)	
SHAPE Round	
MILK Pasteurized cow's	
RENNET Vegetarian	
TYPE Modern	

HARBOURNE BLUE DEVON

Robin Congdon makes this cheese at Ticklemore Cheeses, near Sharpham Barton, one of a trio of blue cheeses made from different milks. The milk used for this cheese comes from a local herd of goats reared outside, which adds complexity and interest to the flavor of their milk, and hence to the cheese. Matured for four months, the ivory paste is streaked with blue-green veining, and it has a fruity, spicy flavor.

SIZE	
D. 8in (20cm)	
H. 4–5in (10–13cm)	
WEIGHT	
6½–7½lb (3–3.5kg)	
SHAPE Round	
MILK Pasteurized goat's	
RENNET Vegetarian	
TYPE Modern	

ISLE OF WIGHT BLUE
ISLE OF WIGHT

This cheese is made by the Isle of Wight Cheese Company using unpasteurized Guernsey milk from the dairy herd at the farm at which it is based. It is sold at four weeks, by which time it has a brown natural rind, blotched with mold, and a smooth creamy-textured paste. It has a nutty flavor and gentle bite from the veining.

SIZE	
D. 3½in (9cm)	
H. 1¾in (4.5cm)	
WEIGHT	
8oz (225g)	
SHAPE Round	
MILK Unpasteurized cow's	
RENNET Vegetarian	
TYPE Modern	

LANARK BLUE LANARKSHIRE

Humphrey Errington makes this cheese at Braehead of Walston using unpasteurized milk from his own ewes. *Penicillium roqueforti* is added to the warm milk at the start of the process. The curd is cut, drained of whey, packed into molds, brined, salt-rubbed, and pierced to encourage the veining, then matured for six weeks. The pale ivory-colored paste is mottled with blue-green veining and has a full, savory flavor.

SIZE	
D. 6½in (16cm)	
H. 4¾in (12cm)	
WEIGHT	
6½lb (3kg)	
SHAPE Wheel	
MILK Unpasteurized sheep's	
RENNET Vegetarian	
TYPE Modern	

MRS BELL'S BLUE YORKSHIRE

This blue sheep's milk cheese is made by Shepherds Purse Cheeses of Thirsk using locally sourced milk, and is named after Judy Bell, who founded the company in 1987 on the Bells' farm. During maturing, the cheese develops a natural rind over a white paste, streaked with emphatic green-blue veins. The texture is soft and creamy with a sweet flavor, and there is only a mild tang from the blueing.

SIZE	
D. 8in (20cm)	
H. 7–8in (18–20 cm)	
WEIGHT	
6½lb (3kg)	
SHAPE Wheel	
MILK Pasteurized sheep's	
RENNET Vegetarian	
TYPE Modern	

NANNY BLOO DEVON

Norsworthy Dairy in Crediton makes this blue cheese using unpasteurized goat's milk from its own mixed herd of Saanen, Toggenburg, and British Alpines. *Penicillium roqueforti* is added to the milk, and the cheese is spiked at three weeks to create the veining. Ready to eat at one month, the cheese has an orange-gold rind and mottled blue-green veining. The paste is soft and moist with a tongue-tingling tangy flavor.

SIZE	
D. 2½in (6cm)	
H. 4in (10cm)	
WEIGHT	
3¼–4lb (1.6–1.8kg)	
SHAPE Cylinder	
MILK Unpasteurized goat's	
RENNET Vegetarian	
TYPE Modern	

NEW FOREST BLUE WILTSHIRE

This blue cheese is made by Loosehanger Farmhouse Cheeses at Home Farm, Salisbury using milk from a single herd of Ayrshires. To create the blue veining, *Penicillium roqueforti* is added to the milk at the start of the process. The cheese is matured for 6–12 weeks, during which time it develops dark blue veining in a moist cream-colored paste, which gives it a pleasant sharpness.

SIZE	
D. 6–6¾in (15–17cm)	
H. 4½in (11cm)	
WEIGHT	
3lb–3lb 3oz (1.3–1.5kg)	
SHAPE Cylinder	
MILK Pasteurized cow's	
RENNET Vegetarian	
TYPE Modern	

OLD SARUM WILTSHIRE

Loosehanger Farmhouse Cheeses makes this blue cheese using pasteurized milk from a single herd of Ayrshires. Taking its inspiration from the sweeter blue cheeses, Loosehanger uses a French version of a *Dolcelatte* mold to create the blueing. Ready to eat at six weeks, the cheese has a grayish-brown natural rind and a yellow paste with green veining. The flavor is sweet and creamy with a gentle blue note.

SIZE	
D. 6–6¾in (15–17cm)	
H. 4½in (11cm)	
WEIGHT	
3lb–3lb 3oz (1.3–1.5kg)	
SHAPE Cylinder	
MILK Pasteurized cow's	
RENNET Vegetarian	
TYPE Modern	

PARTRIDGE'S BLUE SOMERSET

The Exmoor Blue Cheese Company at Willett Farm makes this blue cheese using locally sourced milk from Jersey cows. *Penicillium roqueforti* is added to the milk to create the veining, and the cheese is matured for six to eight weeks. It develops a natural rind over a pale yellow paste, intricately veined with blue-green mold. The texture is soft and creamy, and the flavor is mellow with a savory salty-sweetness.

SIZE	
D. 4½in (11cm)	
H. 4in (10cm)	
WEIGHT	
2½lb (1.1kg)	
SHAPE Drum	
MILK Unpasteurized cow's	
RENNET Vegetarian	
TYPE Modern	

PERL LAS DYFED

An organic blue cheese, this is made by Caws Cenarth at Glyneithinog Farm in Wales using cow's milk from Ffosyficer Organic farm. Matured for at least eight weeks, the cheese grows a pale gold natural rind, flecked with white, while the pale yellow paste is evenly veined with blue-green veining. When ripe, the paste becomes meltingly soft, while the flavor is salty and nutty with a mushroomy note from the veining.

SIZE
D. 4in (10cm) & 8in (20cm)
H. 3¼in (8cm) & 4in (10cm)

WEIGHT
1lb (450g) & 5½lb (2.5kg)

SHAPE Round

MILK Pasteurized organic cow's

RENNET Vegetarian

TYPE Modern

PONT GAR BLUE CARMARTHENSHIRE

This small cheese is made in Wales by the Carmarthenshire Cheese Company based at Boksberg Hall, Llanllwch. It is a white mold-ripened cheese, and when matured, the cheese's golden rind is coated with a bloomy white mold layer, caused by the *Penicillium candidum* added to the cheese. Inside, the glossy ivory-colored paste is marked with a sprinkling of blue veining, adding a tang to the mild-flavored cheese.

SIZE
D. 4in (10cm)
H. 1¼in (3cm)

WEIGHT
9oz (250g)

SHAPE Round

MILK Pasteurized cow's

RENNET Vegetarian

TYPE Modern

QUANTOCK BLUE SOMERSET

The Exmoor Blue Cheese Company at Willett Farm, Lydeard St. Lawrence, makes this blue cheese using locally sourced sheep's milk, to which *Penicillium candidum* is added. Matured for four to six weeks, the cheese has a natural rind over an ivory-colored paste, splotched with green-blue mold. The cheese's texture is crumbly, while the flavor combines the sweet nuttiness of sheep's milk with a blue tang.

SIZE	
D. 4½in (11cm)	
H. 4in (10cm)	
WEIGHT	
2¼lb (1kg)	
SHAPE Drum	
MILK Unpasteurized sheep's	
RENNET Vegetarian	
TYPE Modern	

SHROPSHIRE BLUE
LEICESTERSHIRE

This cheese is not historically linked with Shropshire; it is, in fact, made by a number of the Stilton dairies. Colston Bassett makes the one shown, maturing it for six to eight weeks. Annatto is added to create the orange color, while the veins are produced by adding *Penicillium roqueforti*. It has a firm but moist paste and a subtle, savory flavor.

SIZE	
D. 8in (20cm)	
H. 10in (25cm)	
WEIGHT	
17½lb (8kg)	
SHAPE Cylinder	
MILK Pasteurized cow's	
RENNET Vegetarian	
TYPE Modern	

SOMERSET BLUE SOMERSET

This cheese is made by the Exmoor Blue Cheese Company at Willett Farm, Lydeard St. Lawrence, using Jersey cow's milk sourced locally. The blue veining is created by the addition of *Penicillium candidum*. It is matured for five to six weeks, developing a tracing of blue-green veining through the creamy yellow paste. The texture is yielding, while the spicy blueing contrasts with the butteriness of the rich Jersey milk.

SIZE	
D. 6in (15cm)	
H. 4in (10cm)	
WEIGHT	
4½lb (2kg)	
SHAPE Round	
MILK Unpasteurized cow's	
RENNET Vegetarian	
TYPE Modern	

STICHELTON NOTTINGHAMSHIRE

Randolph Hodgson of Neal's Yard Dairy and cheesemaker Joe Schneider have teamed up to create this blue cheese, made at the Stichelton Dairy, Collingthwaite Farm. Named after the original name of Stilton village, it is made using unpasteurized cow's milk from the farm, and traditional animal rennet. Matured for 12–14 weeks, it has a natural rind, a blue-veined yellow paste, and a savory, lingering flavor.

SIZE	
D. 8in (20cm)	
H. 8½in (22cm)	
WEIGHT	
15½lb (7kg)	
SHAPE Cylinder	
MILK Unpasteurized cow's	
RENNET Traditional animal	
TYPE Modern	

STILTON LEICS, NOTTS, & DERBYS

Stilton, Britain's most famous blue cheese, has a venerable history. It was named after the town of Stilton, where at a busy stagecoach station on the Great North Road, the enterprising landlord of the Bell Inn sold the cheese to appreciative travelers.

In the early 1720s, author Daniel Defoe wrote of passing through Stilton, which was, he noted, a town "famous for cheese." He went on to describe the cheese as follows: "It is called our English Parmesan, and is brought to table with the mites or maggots round it so thick that they bring a spoon with them for you to eat the mites with, as you do the cheese."

The fame of Stilton cheese during this period is attributed in part to Mrs. Frances Pawlett of Wymondham in Leicestershire, a skilled cheesemaker credited with doing much to rationalize the shape, size, and quality of the blue cheese made locally. This blue cheese was then supplied to Cooper Thornhill at the Bell Inn in Stilton, who became noted as the seller of the best blue cheese in the town.

A POPULAR CHEESE

Although the coming of the railways in the 1840s saw the collapse of the stage-coach business, the fame of Stilton cheese had spread, and it went on to attract an appreciative audience in London. It became particularly popular with members of the aristocracy, who visited nearby Melton Mowbray in Leicestershire to hunt. Its status as a staple of English food continues today, as Stilton remains a much-loved cheese across Britain and beyond, with national sales peaking at Christmas time.

COLSTON BASSETT STILTON

SIZE	
D. 8in (20cm)	
H. 7½in (19.5cm)	
WEIGHT	
17–17½ lb (7.8–8kg)	
SHAPE Cylinder	
MILK Pasteurized cow's	
RENNET Traditional animal or vegetarian	
TYPE Traditional	

made using animal or vegetable rennet

balance of flavors between blue veining and curd

creamy texture

COLSTON BASSETT STILTON

Among the smallest Stilton dairies, Colston Bassett near Nottingham has sourced its milk from the same farms since 1913. Great care is taken hand-ladling the curds into molds. Matured for at least eight weeks, this Stilton has a mellow flavor and a hallmark creaminess.

A PROTECTED CHEESE

Unusually in the history of British cheeses, Stilton cheese was defined and protected early in the 20th century. In 1910, a group of Stilton cheesemakers set out a definitive process for making the cheese, and in 1969, when the cheesemakers sought legal protection for this method, a High Court judgment ruled as follows: "Stilton is a blue or white cheese made from full cream milk, with no applied pressure, forming its own crust or coat, and made in cylindrical form, the milk coming from English dairy herds in the district of Melton Mowbray and the surrounding areas of Leicestershire, Derbyshire, and Nottinghamshire."

Today, Stilton has the distinction of being one of the few British cheeses to be granted a Protected Designation Origin (PDO) status by the European Union. It must be made by only a licensed dairy in the counties of Derbyshire, Leicestershire, or Nottinghamshire from local pasteurized milk in a traditional cylindrical shape. It must be made according to a traditional recipe, never pressed, and allowed to form its own crust. There are only seven UK dairies producing Stilton: Colston Bassett, Cropwell Bishop, Dairy Crest, Long Clawson, Quenby Hall, Tuxford & Tebbutt, and Websters. Together they produce more than a million Stilton cheeses each year.

THE PRODUCTION PROCESS

It takes 137 pints (78 liters) of milk to make one 17½lb (8kg) Stilton cheese. At the start of the process, the milk is mixed with a starter culture, a milk-clotting agent, and blue-mold spores (*Penicillium roqueforti*). The resulting curd is drained, cut, milled, and salted, and for each cheese, around 24lb (11kg) of salted curd is placed in a cylindrical mold. This is drained naturally for five or six days, and turned daily to spread the moisture evenly. Crucially, Stilton is never pressed during the making process, allowing the cheese to develop the flaky, open texture essential for the blueing stage.

The drained cheeses are then sealed and ripened for a number of weeks, again being turned regularly; during this period, they begin to form the classic Stilton crust. At about six weeks, the cheeses are pierced with long needles, allowing air to enter and the *Penicillum roqueforti* mold to grow, creating the characteristic blue-green veining. The Stilton cheeses leave the dairy at nine weeks, by which time their weight has reduced to around 17½lb (8kg) a cheese. The resulting Stilton has a blotched crust, a blue-veined paste, and a crumbly texture with a lasting, savory taste. Longer maturing, for another five to six weeks, results in a creamier texture and a mellower, fuller flavor. Although all seven Stilton dairies use the same overall techniques, the resulting cheeses vary noticeably in flavor and texture from dairy to dairy.

CROPWELL BISHOP STILTON
NOTTINGHAMSHIRE

Named after the village in which it is based, Cropwell Bishop Creamery sources the milk for its cheese from 10 core farms, with *Penicillium roqueforti* added to create the blueing. At its peak at 11 weeks, it has a distinctive pattern of blue-green veining with a rich but not overly assertive spicy flavor. Cropwell Bishop also produces an organic Stilton.

SIZE	
D. 8in (20cm)	
H. 10in (25cm)	
WEIGHT	
17½lb (8kg)	
SHAPE Cylinder	
MILK Pasteurized cow's	
RENNET Vegetarian	
TYPE Traditional	

QUENBY HALL STILTON
LEICESTERSHIRE

During the 18th century, the owner of Quenby Hall made a blue cheese that was sold in Stilton. The current owner, Freddie de Lisle, has revived the tradition. Matured for up to 12 weeks, it has a textured natural rind and a firm yellow paste, mottled with blue-green veining. The texture is creamy and the flavor is mild with a nutty tang.

SIZE	
D. 8¼in (21cm)	
H. 10in (25 cm)	
WEIGHT	
17½–20lb (8–9kg)	
SHAPE Cylinder	
MILK Pasteurized cow's	
RENNET Vegetarian	
TYPE Traditional	

STRATHDON BLUE ROSS-SHIRE

This blue cheese is made by Highland Fine Cheeses at Tain in Scotland. In order to retain the moisture in the curd, it is not scalded at all. The molded cheese is matured for three months, developing a mold rind from the yeast still in the air from the dairy building's past as a brewery. It is a mild blue with a pale, moist veined paste, developing a long, peppery finish when older.

SIZE	
D. 12in (30cm)	
H. 4in (10cm)	
WEIGHT	
6¼lb (2.8kg)	
SHAPE Round	
MILK Pasteurized cow's	
RENNET Traditional animal & vegetarian	
TYPE Modern	

SUFFOLK BLUE SUFFOLK

The Suffolk Cheese Company makes this cheese using pasteurized milk from its herd of Guernsey cows and adding *Penicillium roqueforti* at the start of the making process. The unpressed, molded curd is horizontally pierced and allowed to mature until it is four to five weeks old. The rich yellow of the Guernsey milk is reflected in the color of the moist paste, while the flavor is creamy with a mellow blue note.

SIZE	
D. 4in (10cm)	
H. 3in (7.5cm)	
WEIGHT	
1½lb (675g)	
SHAPE Round	
MILK Pasteurized cow's	
RENNET Vegetarian	
TYPE Modern	

YORKSHIRE BLUE YORKSHIRE

Shepherds Purse Cheeses in Thirsk makes this blue cheese using locally sourced cow's milk. *Penicillium roqueforti* is added to the milk at the start of the cheese-making process to create the veining. Matured for 10 weeks, the Yorkshire Blue develops a natural rind over a pale yellow paste with blue-green veining. The texture is soft and creamy, and the cheese has a mellow flavor with a salty-nutty finish.

SIZE	
D. 8in (20cm)	
H. 8in (20cm)	
WEIGHT	
6½lb (3kg)	
SHAPE Round	
MILK Pasteurized cow's	
RENNET Vegetarian	
TYPE Modern	

ORGANIC CHEESES

The rise of interest in and demand for organic foods has led to an increasing number of organically certified cheeses being made in the United Kingdom. Whereas in 1994 only four organic cheeses were entered for the British Cheese Awards (see page 185), by 2007 there were 113 entries. For a cheese to be organic, it is not enough for it simply to be made from organic milk. The word "organic" is protected by EU law and covers both the raw materials and the processing, so the word is applied to how the cheese is made as well as what it is made from.

The Soil Association promotes sustainable organic farming and is the UK's largest organic certification body. Organic products must include no genetically modified (GM) organisms or their derivatives. Rennet produced from GM bacteria or fungi, therefore, is not permitted by the Soil Association, which stipulates that organic cheeses must use animal rennet or naturally occurring vegetarian rennet. It is possible to make organic cheeses using traditional calf rennet from non-organic calves.

GLOSSARY

Affinage: the process of ripening or maturing a cheese.

Annatto: a food coloring from seeds of the annatto tree (*Bixa orellana*), traditionally used to add an orange color to cheeses such as Red Leicester or Cheshire.

Biodynamic: a form of organic farming based on a holistic and spiritual understanding of nature.

Brevibacterium linens: an important surface-ripening bacteria used in cheesemaking.

Brining: soaking the cheese in a brine solution.

Curd: the solids created when the milk has been curdled.

Direct vat inoculation: freeze-dried starter cultures used to trigger the cheese-making process, which are added directly to the vat.

Geotrichum candidum: one of the molds used to develop flavor and texture in cheese.

Lactic acid: the weak acid formed by the action of bacteria on lactose.

Lactose: sugar found naturally in milk.

Milling: the process of breaking the curd into small pieces.

Mold-ripened: a cheese into which molds are introduced to develop flavor and texture during ripening.

Protected Designation of Origin (PDO): a European Union system to protect a regional food produced in a given geographical area.

Protected Geographical Indication (PGI): a European Union system to protect a regional food with a link to a given geographical area.

Organic: a food sold as "organic" must be produced according to European laws on organic production, with growers, processors, and importers registered and approved by organic certification bodies.

Paste: the term used to describe the inside of a cheese.

Pasteurized: a term for milk that has been heat-treated, usually by heating it to 161°F (71.7°C) for 15 seconds, to kill naturally occurring micro-organisms that may cause disease.

Penicillium candidum: a mold used to create a bloomy white coating on cheese rinds. Also known as *Penicillium camemberti*.

Penicillium glaucum: a mold that is added to blue cheeses to create the blue-green veins.

Penicillium roqueforti: a mold added to create the blue-green veins in blue cheeses.

Pressing: a process during cheese-making when weight is applied to a molded cheese to extract moisture and create texture.

Raw: describes milk that has not been heat-treated in any way.

Rennet: a substance used to curdle milk, made from animal, vegetarian, or genetically modified sources.

Scalding: heating the curd during cheese-making.

Starter: a mixture of bacteria used to raise the acid levels in milk.

Thermized: a method of heat-treating milk to kill any pathogens in it, using temperatures lower than pasteurization. The term applies to raw milk that has been heated for at least 15 seconds at a temperature between 135°F (57°C) and 154°F (68°C).

Thermophilic: literally "heat-loving," the term is used to describe both a heat-tolerant bacterial starter used in cheeses with a high cooking temperature, and a Swiss-style type of cheese made using such starters.

Traditional pint starter: a frozen bacterial culture that must be diluted and incubated before use. It is added to milk to trigger the first stages of the cheese-making process.

Triple-cream: describes soft cheeses made from milk with extra cream added.

Unpasteurized: a term to describe milk that has not been heat-treated in any way.

Washed-curd: describes a type of cheese made by washing the curd during the making process.

Washed-rind: a type of cheese made by washing the rind during maturing.

Whey: the watery element that remains liquid after milk has been curdled.

DIRECTORY OF RESOURCES

SPECIALIST CHEESE RETAILERS

UNITED STATES
Artisan Cheese Gallery
12023 Ventura Blvd
Studio City, CA 91604
(818) 505-0207

Bedford Cheese Co
111 Deery St
Shelbyville, TN 37160
(931) 684-5422
(615) 898-0662
www.bedfordcheese.com

Bon Appetit
301 N Harrison St
Princeton, NJ 08540
(609) 924-7755
www.bonappetitfinefoods.com

The British Pantry Ltd
8125 161st Ave NE
Redmond, WA 98052
(425) 883-7511
www.thebritishpantryltd.com

Cavaniola Gourmet Cheese
89B Division St
Sag Harbor, NY 11963
(631) 725-0095

Chalet Wine & Cheese Shop
3000 N Clark St
Chicago, IL 60657
(773) 935-9400

The Cheese Company
5575 E 3rd Ave
Denver, CO 80220
(303) 394-9911

The Cheese House
1336 Foothill Dr
Salt Lake City, UT 84108
(801) 582-7758

Cheese Importers
33 S Pratt Pkwy
Longmont, CO 80501
(303) 772-4444
www.cheeseimporters.com

The Cheese Store of Beverly Hills
419 N Beverly Dr
Beverly Hills, CA 90210
(310) 278-2855
www.cheesestorebh.com

Cheesetique Specialty Cheese
2403 Mount Vernon Ave
Alexandria, VA 22301
(703) 706-5300
www.cheesetique.com

Chestnut Hill Cheese Shop
8509 Germantown Ave
Philadelphia, PA 19118
(215) 242-2211
www.chcheeseshop.com

Di Bruno Brothers
1730 Chestnut St
Philadelphia, PA 19103
(215) 665-9220
www.dibruno.com

Eastman Party Store
5205 Eastman Ave
Midland, MI 48640
(989) 835-7991
www.eastmanpartystore.com

Eastside Marketplace Inc
165 Pitman St
Providence, RI 02906
(401) 831-7771
(401) 831-5370
www.eastsidemarket.com

**Foster & Dobbs
Authentic Foods**
2518 15th Avenue NE
Portland, OR 97212
(503) 284-1157
(503) 284-1158
www.fosteranddobbs.com

Frogs Breath Cheese Store
143 N Glassell
Orange, CA 92866
(714) 744-1773
www.frogsbreathcheese.com

**Heini's Cheese Chalet &
Country Mall**
Millersburg, OH 44654
(330) 893-2131
(800) 253-6636
(330) 893-2079
www.heinis.com

**Pastoral Artisan Cheese,
Bread & Wine**
53 E Lake St
Chicago, IL 60601
(312) 658-1250
www.pastoralartisan.com

Mr Marcel's Gourmet Market
6333 W 3rd St # 236
Los Angeles, CA 90036
(323) 939-7792
www.farmersmarketla.com

Murray's Cheese
254 Bleecker St
New York, NY 10014
(212) 243-3289
www.murrayscheese.com

DIRECTORY OF RESOURCES

Nicole's Gourmet Food
921 Meridian Ave # B
South Pasadena, CA 91030
(626) 403-5751
www.nicolesgourmetfoods.com

Surdyk's
303 E Hennepin Ave
Minneapolis, MN 55414
(612) 379-3232
(612) 379-7511
www.surdyks.com

Taste Artisan Cheese & Gourmet Shop
1243 University Ave
San Diego, CA 92103
 (619) 683-2306
www.tastecheese.com

Truffle
2906 E 6th Ave
Denver, CO 80206
(303) 322-7363
www.denvertruffle.com

Village Gourmet Cheese and Wine Shop
4357 Tujunga Ave
Studio City, CA 91604
(818) 487-3807
www.villagegourmetcheese
andwine.com

Wasik's Cheese Shop
61 Central St
Wellesley, MA 02482
(781) 237-0916
www.wasiks.com

CANADA
All the Best Fine Foods Ltd
1101 Yonge ST
Toronto, ON M4W 2L7, Canada
www.allthebestfinefoods.com

Dairy Capital Cheese Shoppe
474 Dundas Street
Woodstock, ON N4S 1C4, Canada
(519) 537-7623
www.dairycapitalcheese.ca

Family Gourmet Deli Encore Foods Ltd
Suite 143, 1199 Lynn Valley Road
North Vancouver, BC V7J 3H2, Canada
(604) 980-4121

Gourmet Cheese Platters
19 Jutland Road
Etobicoke, ON M8Z 2G6, Canada
(416) 248-6539

Gourmet Cheese Shoppe
3905 Don Mills Road
North York, ON M2H 2S7, Canada
(416) 491-2859

ON-LINE MAIL-ORDER RETAILERS

www.artisanalcheese.com

A broad selection of British and other European cheeses and wines.

www.cheesesupply.com

Over 700 cheeses, including British varieties. Delivers to United States.

www.cheesestorebh.com

Purveyors of fine cheeses, wines, and other luxury foods.

www.cowgirlcreamery.com

Artisan cheesemakers who also sell European cheeses by mail-order.

www.formaggiokitchen.com

Sells cheeses, including classic British varieties, and other fine foods.

www.gourmetfoodstore.com

Delivers cheese and fine foods to mainland United States only.

www.idealcheese.com

Cheeses and other gourmet items delivered within the United States.

www.igourmet.com

A wide range of gourmet foods delivered within the United States.

OTHER SOURCES OF INFORMATION

The British Cheese Board

29–35 Lexington Street
London W1F 9AH
+44 117 921 1744
www.cheeseboard.co.uk

The Irish Farmhouse Cheesemakers Association

www.irishcheese.ie

The Reluctant Gourmet

www.reluctantgourmet.com

Slow Food

www.slowfood.com

Specialist Cheesemakers' Association

17 Clerkenwell Green
London EC1R 0DP
+44 20 7253 2114
www.specialistcheesemakers.co.uk

Stilton Cheesemakers' Association

www.stiltoncheese.com

West Country Farmhouse Cheesemakers

www.farmhousecheesemakers.com

INDEX

INDEX

BIBLIOGRAPHY

Clifford, Sue & King, Angela, *England in Particular*, Hodder & Stoughton, London 2006

Davidson, Alan, *The Oxford Companion to Food*, Oxford University Press, Oxford, 1999

Freeman, Sarah, *The Real Cheese Companion*, Little, Brown & Company, London, 1998

Harbutt, Juliet, *Cheese*, Mitchell Beazley, London, 1999

Harbutt, Juliet, *Cheeses of the World*, Hermes House, London, 1999

Hickman, Trevor, *The History of Stilton Cheese*, Sutton Publishing, Stroud, 2005

Mason, Laura with Brown, Catherine, *Traditional Foods of Britain*, Prospect Books, Totnes, 1999

Masui, Kazuko & Yamada, Tomoko, *French Cheeses*, Dorling Kindersley, London, 1996

Michelson, Patricia, *The Cheese Room*, Penguin, London, 2005

Rance, Patrick, *The Great British Cheese Book*, Papermac, London, 1985

ACKNOWLEDGMENTS

My heartfelt thanks, first of all, to the cheesemakers themselves, for their time and trouble in assisting me with this book, and also to the many wonderful cheesemongers and delicatessens who were fantastically helpful: Ian of the Cheese Shed; Elise and Gary Jungheim of Country Cheeses; the Fine Cheese Company; Patricia Michelson and Sarah Bilney at La Fromagerie; Mark Newman and Will Johnston of Hamish Johnston; Marc Kennard of Kennards; Randolph Hodgson and his great team at Neals Yard Dairy, with special thanks to Chris George, Michael Jones, Bronwen Percival, Sarah Stewart, and Martin Tkalez; Paxton and Whitfield; Philip and Karen Rippon and Jeremy of Rippon Cheese Stores; and Kevin Sheridan of Sheridan's Cheesemongers in Ireland. Putting a book together involves a lot of work from several people. My thanks for all their help and support to: Dawn Bates, Emma Forge and Tom Forge, Adèle Hayward, Will Heap, Stephanie Jackson, Kat Mead, Daniel Mills, Samantha Richards, Sara Robin, Siobhan Vorney, and Jenny Woodcock.

DK would like to thank Will Heap and Siobhan Vorney for their work on photography; Randolph Hodgson and his team for permission to photograph at Neal's Yard Dairy; and Sonia Mahabir for compiling the resources.